BUTTER & CHEESEMAKING

V. Cheke &
A. Sheppard

BUTTER & CHEESE MAKING

Edited and with
a Foreword by
K. D. Maddever

Line drawings
by Peter Haillay

ALPHABOOKS

First published as *Cheese and Butter* in 1956
Alphabooks revised edition 1980
Designed, produced and published by Alphabet and Image Ltd,
Sherborne, Dorset, England

ISBN: 0 906670 00 4 (cloth)
      0 906670 14 4 (paper)

Printed in Britain by T.J. Press (Padstow) Ltd., Padstow,
Cornwall

All line drawings by Peter Haillay

Cover photograph by Bob Marchant

CONTENTS

FOREWORD

There are few books which set out the basic technology in Dairying: *Cheese and Butter* written by V.Cheke and A.Sheppard is one. As a student of dairying at the University of Reading I had the privilege of being taught by these ladies of outstanding ability. They were so well informed and so practical it is not surprising that their book contains a wealth of information of prime importance to anyone who wishes to try his or her hand at cream, butter or cheese-making.

Today there is so much interest in self-sufficiency and so many people are trying to cope with small quantities of surplus milk, I am sure the reprinting of this book will be well worthwhile.

Although techniques in the manufacture of dairy products on a commercial scale are being constantly changed and updated the data given in this book must be applied however much the method is changed.

Cheese-making is both an art and a craft, for the raw material is inevitably of variable chemical composition, depending on the feeding management of the cows and the subsequent treatment of the milk. There are, however, three points which need emphasis, so that much time may be saved and the quality of the finished product be assured. First one must emphasise that any milk from a cow which has been treated for mastitis may contain anti-biotics, which will inhibit the growth of 'starter' organisms—this would completely upset the cheese-making process. Secondly, milk which has been 'Pasteurised' is subject to a change in the calcium salts, and it will not so readily form a coagulum or junket with rennet, therefore about 50% extra rennet must be used. Thirdly one cannot emphasise too often that cleanliness in the production of milk will ensure a product which is bacteriologically clean and of good flavour. Combined with careful production methods one must strive for bacteriologically clean utensils, both metal and wooden ones, and here the vital points are the following: rinse first in cold water, scrub in hot detergent and finally 'scald' with actively BOILING water. If chemical sterilants are used (usually containing chlorine) they must be of correct strength and be given an adequate contact time of 2-3 minutes. There is a great deal of valuable information in Chapter 1 and I would strongly advise, beginners in particular, to read this section very carefully. Since the book was first published metrication has been introduced, so for the benefit of readers, tables have been included which should be used in conjunction with the text throughout.

K.D.Maddever 1980
Formerly Regional Dairy Husbandry Adviser A.D.A.S.

INTRODUCTION

This book is not intended to be a technological treatise on the manufacture of cheese, whether on the true 'cheese-making farms' or in the creameries. Farmhouse cheese-making has become an industrialised craft, and is decreasingly individual as economic pressures necessitate centralisation of plant and labour.

Creamery manufacture, with its bulk handling and standardised methods, is an industrial branch of dairying. Modern methods of manufacture are so much involved with chemistry, microbiology and mechanisation, that specific text books would be required to deal with any one part of the process.

This book is essentially for the ordinary consumer: the farmer's wife, the housewife, or any person in town or country who may be interested. It deals with the economical use of the smaller amount of milk, either that which is unsold surplus from the farm, or purchased especially for the purposes of home manufacture. It considers the subject from the craftsman's point of view, but allows for those modern innovations which can be helpful without unduly complicating the processes.

It cannot hope to cover the methods of manufacturing the orthodox types of hard-pressed cheese, such as large Cheddar and Cheshire. These are not suitable for small scale work, as they require a big gallonage of milk, and much more equipment than can be considered here. It describes a few types of semi-hard and soft cheeses, and some of the acid-curd varieties. All these can be made from small, fluctuating amounts of milk, up to ten gallons in quantity. They do not require expensive outlay on apparatus, and can be made in the farmhouse, or home, where no routine cheese-making equipment is available.

It is hoped to show that with reasonable precautions and by intelligent modifications, no great expense need be involved. Milk which might otherwise be wasted, or fed to stock on the farm, can be used instead to provide food for the household, or products for sale.

The householder who does not live on, or have access to, a farm, may consider it worth while to buy some extra milk for manufacturing purposes.

The basic principles concerned with cheese manufacture, and the methods applied to the types of cheese concerned, are dealt with separately. This makes it easier to interpret the specific details of the cheese recipes, which follow the general descriptions. The term cheese recipe itself is a misleading one, because too many factors are involved to guarantee any positive result. Everyone knows that a cookery recipe is not infallible, because of the variations in the mixing, baking and individual handling. Most of the cooking ingredients are standard, but in cheese-making, the initial milk can be infinitely varied. For this reason the simplest process can be upset by a chemical or biological factor in the milk. Undesired fermentations may be caused by the presence of the wrong type of micro-organisms, and the cheese produced may be abnormal, even if the recipe has been accurately followed. There is in fact plenty of scope for the true craftsman, who can develop the inherent senses of taste, smell and touch, and use his commonsense as well. He can learn to distinguish the variations in milk and curd, which require a change in the methods of handling if he is to avert disaster. He can assess the general quality of milk by its taste and smell, distinguishing bad flavours as taints, and good flavour by its 'cleanness'. He can judge the relative acidity in milk or curd by the same means, and form his own methods for successful manufacture. He can feel the texture of the curd, and judge its degree of firmness, softness and mellowness. Even with practice, there remains in cheese-making a degree of hit-or-miss, and in order to prevent excessive loss simple precautions are recommended

The element of uncertainty exists even when expert cheese makers employ all the modern methods of standardising, mechanisation and scientific control. This seems to prove that in spite of all the technical innovations that have been made, cheese-making remains a craft. There is therefore no reason why the amateur should fail, provided he keeps to simple methods. Cream production and butter-making are less complex concerns, though many of the same general rules apply. The final chapters describe the methods suitable to the small farm, and for the home, when it is wished to enjoy the various creams, cream 'cheese', and genuine 'farmhouse' butter.

1 WHAT'S IN A CHEESE

Cheese has formed a stable part of the human diet for many centuries, and references to its manufacture are to be found in early classical literature. Descriptions also occur in many old British books, especially in those dealing with farm practice in specific areas of England, Scotland and Wales.

In countries with a hot climate, where milk has a very short keeping quality, curds and cheese are a means of avoiding wastage. They also provide a nutritious and concentrated form of the milk constituents. They have good storage properties, for the reduced moisture allows the product to keep for longer periods without deterioration. Many tropical and sub-tropical countries possess national milk-drinks and foods, the recipes for which have been handed down from generation to generation. These preparations are based on lactic acid fermentation, which is the natural 'souring' of milk. Some of them are consumed as curds, and others as drinks with varying contents of acid and alcohol, the latter being produced by certain yeasts which are present with the bacteria. It is interesting to note that in countries where intestinal disorders are most

liable to occur, the therapeutic value of soured milk preparations has for long been realised. This fact has been commercialised in Europe, and to some extent in Britain, by the manufacture and sale of products such as yoghurt, and various proprietary curd cheeses. These are fermented by special cultures of organisms, grown for the purpose, but are of similar basic type to those found in the mixed ones used in South European and Eastern countries. The lactic acid fermentation is known as the 'normal' one for milk, as it occurs spontaneously unless there is some heavy contamination from undesirable types of bacteria. The 'souring' organisms produce lactic acid by fermentation of the milk-sugar, or lactose, and when sufficient acidity is produced, it will coagulate the casein (the organic compound forming the basis of cheese), causing the familiar curdling of sour milk. Yeasts should not be present, as in the lactic acid plus alcohol fermentations. In milk for cheese-making, yeasts are undesirable contaminants.

Straightforward lactic acid fermentation is used in all forms of cheese-making, but it is essential to distinguish the two basic forms of curd. The curd formed by acid-coagulation of the casein (souring) can be used for making a number of acid-curd and curd/cream preparations, but cannot be used for the true cheeses such as Cheddar, Stilton, etc. The latter require a basic curd formed from coagulation of the casein by the action of rennet. During the subsequent manufacture, lactic acid fermentation is used, as the souring organisms continue to ferment the milk sugar to form lactic acid. This acid has specific actions on the rennet-curd, and by varying the amount of acidity, and using different methods of handling the curd, it is possible to make many types and varieties of cheese from the same initial milk supply. This fact refutes the assumption that specific varieties of cheese can only be made in their local areas of origin. Probably this common error has arisen because it often seems that localised conditions of soil and herbage favour the manufacture of certain varieties. There is no scientific reason to support the claim, but it is obvious that the milk produced off soils of varying composition will be influenced in its chemical and physical properties, and so affect the curd and cheese made from it.

Consumption of cheese

Countries vary enormously in their consumption of cheese per head of the population. This is partly due to geographical and climatic factors, but is chiefly influenced by economic ones. The British are comparatively low on the cheese consumer list, probably because the main part of the population is concentrated in towns. Consumption is found to be highest in those countries where a basic proportion of the population is composed of self-employed farmers, as such families are economically forced to be as self-supporting as possible. This accounts for the large number of local cheeses made in Europe, and in other countries, where many villages, and even farmsteads, have originated their own proprietary cheeses. Cheese which is surplus to family requirements is sent to the local market.

Some of the 'local' cheeses have been put into large scale production, such as the famous Camembert cheese. Considerable quantities of many varieties are exported and are to be found in delicatessens and general produce stores.

The methods of production, and custom of consumption, of cheese on the British farms have always differed greatly from the continental. The traditional British method embodies the manufacture of large sized cheeses, with long storage properties. Those surplus to the market requirements are regarded as part of the family food store. The large cheese is something to 'cut at', and forms a nutritious food during all seasons of the year. There are still some farms where cheese is specially kept for issue as rations during hay and harvest times. At one time it was a general custom for the table to be graced with an entire cheese. It might be a ten-pound Loaf or Truckle, or a fifty-to-eighty pounder, and was of the variety local to the district. The cheese stood on a platter of wood or earthenware, and as it was passed round from man to man, wedges of cheese were cut out by each consumer. The tradition survives on some farms where cheese-making is still practised, though social changes have modified the custom to a home and family affair, the communal table for farm workers being seldom seen. It is regret-

table that the modern conditions of life have jeopardised the chances of survival of many of the ancient farmhouse customs and routines of farm practice. At one time the cheese-maker, and his cheese, were of sufficient importance to be the subject of traditional lore, as exemplified by tales and customs still in existence.

In spite of the changes in farm and national economy, with the inevitable centralisation demanded by modern industry, cheese-making has continued as a fluctuating, but still important branch of the dairy industry. Manufacture has mainly been concentrated in certain areas, such as Cheshire, South Wales, Somerset, Dorset, and some of the Midland counties. In spite of changes in agricultural policy, in world import and export prices, and in social conditions, some of these 'territorial' cheese varieties are still made on the farms.

The demands of the large industrial population have required the import of large amounts of foreign cheese, and at times it seems that the famous British farmhouse cheese may be in danger of extinction. The comparative advantages of selling milk to a distributor are obvious to the farmer, for he receives a guaranteed price, and has no further responsibility after it leaves the farm gate.

In past years farm cheese-making was chiefly in the hands of the farmers' wives and daughters, aided by 'dairymaids' from the village who were hired seasonally. The women were content to do the arduous work, most of which occurred during the summer months. Social changes have reduced the appeal of life and work on the home farm, while the farmer's wife is tied by home and family affairs for which she can

11

seldom obtain help. The one-time dairymaids now drift to the towns, so that any large-scale farmhouse cheese-maker must usually import expensive labour. The general trend in the last thirty years has consequently been towards bulk manufacture of cheese in 'creameries' or factories, with the production of a relatively standard type of cheese. The complete elimination of the farm cheese-maker has only been prevented by the special subsidy schemes, but in spite of all efforts there has been a big decline in the number of farms engaged in cheese-making.

Nowadays, the farmer's wife, or the housewife, who can obtain the necessary milk, can quite economically ring the changes in the family diet by making small cheeses in the home. The prevention of waste with small quantities of surplus milk on the farm, or in the home, is quite a frequent problem, and one which must be solved quickly by somebody on the spot. It is not always possible to obtain the necessary advice just when required, though the British farmer's wife has the advantage of being able to contact official Advisory Officers. Dairy Husbandry Advisers of A.D.A.S.* are available to advise on problems connected with utilisation of surplus milk, and the manufacture of home-made farm products. The A.D.A.S. Officers are chiefly concerned with the statutory regulations and hygienic control of milk production on the farm, and though willing and able to advise on other matters, they are busy members of the Civil Service and should not be asked to spare precious time on minor matters connected with the use of milk.

*A.D.A.S. (Agricultural Development and Advisory Services) M.A.F.F.

Terminology and classification*

There is much confusion in terminology, and the word 'cheese' is so loosely used that even a technical expert may find it difficult to define the variations.

If the innumerable foreign types and varieties are omitted from any list, there still remain many classes of British products which come under the heading of cheese. The time is due when some more definite classification should be made, as at present members both of the industry and of the public, are often at a loss to know in which group any one cheese should belong. A fundamental weakness is the absence of any defined compositional analyses, other than a minimum fat content required in graded cheese. A number of hybrid products can be sold as specific types of cheese, and may additionally be labelled with misleading names. There are no guarantees of fat or protein

*The British Cheese Regulations 1970 No 94. came into operation on 31 January 1970. These set out composition and description of hard, soft, whey, processed cheese and cheese spread. Anyone making cheese for sale must consult this Statutory Instrument re. composition and labelling.

contents, and providing the product can safely pass the Food and Drugs Act the public has no means of knowing exactly what they are buying. The following list gives a rough grouping of the types and varieties of British cheeses, and is intended to provide some clarification of the confused position, in so far as it is possible. It cannot include the numerous proprietary products, which may come into any of the categories. It must also be remembered that many of the territorial names, such as Cheddar, are now in world-wide use and can therefore be used for cheese not made in Britain, such as New Zealand and American Cheddar. The grading schemes for British Farmhouse, and British Creamery, cheese, should prevent confusion on this issue. These grade marks are stamped on the cheese, and define its quality as well as its British origin. Membership of British grading schemes is voluntary, and applies only to farm and creamery manufacturers, who are licensed makers in these schemes. The absence of grade marks does not therefore denote that a cheese is of foreign origin. Much British cheese is sold ungraded and unmarked, and must then rely on its own individual reputation of quality for stimulation of sale.

Group 1: **Hard-pressed cheese** British varieties of territorial cheese.*

Cheddar. English or Scottish. Cylindrical shape, weight 50-90lb.

Cheddar. Truckle or Loaf. Cylindrical shape, weight 8-12lb. English cheese uncoloured. Scottish cheese sometimes coloured.

*Most of the varieties listed are now produced in film wrapped rectangular blocks weighing 41-42lbs.

Cheshire. Cylindrical shape, weight 50-90lb. Truckle or Loaf, cylindrical shape. Weight 8-12lb. Coloured or uncoloured.

Leicester. Flat shape. Weight 40lb. Deeply coloured.

Derby. Flat shape. Weight 30lb. Uncoloured, or lightly coloured.

Double Gloucester. Half-cylinder. Weight 28-40lb. Uncoloured or lightly coloured.

Single Gloucester. Flat shape. Weight 15-25lb. Uncoloured.

Lancashire. Half cylinder. Weight 25-40lb. Uncoloured.

Scottish Dunlop. Flat shape. Weight 28-40lb. Uncoloured.

These hard-pressed cheeses are made from full cream cow's milk, and can be produced on specially-equipped cheese farms, or in creameries. They are types which will store for varying periods, according to their ripening properties and the amount of flavour required to be developed for market. They undergo a period of ripening on the manufacturer's premises, and are mostly cut up at the retailer's for ultimate sale. When any cheese is ripened to its optimum point, it should possess the characteristic flavour for that variety. Much of the best Farmhouse Cheddar is now matured for 6-12 months, but the expense involved in long periods of storage has resulted in a majority of cheese receiving a minimum ripening. This short period is succeeded by low temperature storage to avoid spoiling, and the development

Double Gloucester

Leicester

14

of flavour is checked. Consequently a great deal of cheese is distributed while still comparatively immature. This suits some varieties and some markets where it is in constant demand, but is a detrimental practice when a variety of cheese is at its best with a fully developed flavour.

Flavour can only develop if time is allowed for ripening, and when time is money, the frequent result is the sale of mild, dull-flavoured cheese.

The large territorial cheeses are of necessity cut up at the retailer's premises. This can cause considerable wastage, and drying-out of individual cut portions of cheese. The distributive trade is consequently much concerned with modern methods of packaging cut portions. Wrappings which are moisture- and air-proof are already on the market, but to be absolutely effective, air in the package must be drawn out before the wrapping is sealed. This increases cost, owing to the special vacuum plant required, but the wrapped cheese will not spoil. Wrapping in films or foils will protect for a limited time, but moulds will soon grow under the wrap unless it is of special composition. It is easiest to package new cheese, or mild-flavoured cheese made for the purpose, and this method is adopted for many American packs. The packaging of cut portions from a mature full-flavoured British cheese is a difficult matter and provides some technical problems. These are rapidly being overcome, and it should be possible to buy a wrapped portion of mature Farmhouse cheese which will retain its good properties.

Group 2: **Semi-hard cheese** British Varieties. All made from rennet-curds.

Miniature Cheddar and Cheshire. Cylindrical shape, weight 1-2lb. Uncoloured, or coloured. Cylindrical or flat shape, weight 4-8lb.

Caerphilly. Flat shape, weight 7lb. Uncoloured.

'Washed Curd' types. Flat, rounded edges, weight 1-7lb.

Pressed Farm Cheese ('Smallholder'). Cylindrical or flat shape, weight 3-7lb.

The semi-hard varieties are not suitable for prolonged storage, and are consumed when comparatively new. They do not develop a defined 'cheesey' flavour, but are mild, and sometimes slightly acid. They are admirably suited to the small scale manufacturer, and can be used for home consumption or for economic sale. To obtain the best results, full cream milk should be used.

Group 3: **Blue veined cheese** This group contains many famous cheeses, such as Roquefort and Gorgonzola, as well as the modern commercial varieties imported in large amounts into Britain. The surviving British representatives are Stilton, Blue Wensleydale and Blue Vinney. All these have a deserved reputation for a unique type of flavour, and are famous the world over, but unfortunately the stresses of modern economy have made their individual farm-manufacture a rarity. The creamery manufacture on a large scale has meant the development of rapid methods of ripening, by the inoculation of mould spores into the milk or curd. This frequently means that the modern Blue Cheese, of foreign or British growth, lacks the mellow defined flavour of the original varieties. There may be a copious mould growth, but it is growing in a cheese (under three months old) which has

not had time to ripen to its best point. When cheese is 'blued' by natural means, the mould development is slow, and may take 6-9 months. The protein and fat are gradually changed by the ripening process to give the characteristic flavour, much of it being due to action of the moulds.

If cheese is required to blue it must be manufactured in such a way that the curds contain sufficient moisture, acidity and entrapped air in the texture. Subsequently the cheese is stored in a very humid atmosphere, such as in a damp cellar or natural cave. All these factors encourage mould growth. The specific mould (*Penicillium Roqueforti*) is abundant in the humid atmospheres prevalent in the British Isles, as can be proved by leaving a piece of bread to go mouldy. This is the same blue mould as developed in the veined cheese, and at one time the farmhouse cheesemaker sprinkled crumbs of mouldy bread into the curd as an 'inoculation'. The modern creamery manufacturer grows special cultures of the mould in the laboratory, often using bread crumbs as the medium, and adds the mould spores, or 'seeds', to the curd. The way in which the mould grows in a cheese depends on its method of making. Stilton cheese should have a 'marbled' appearance throughout the interior, formed by a dense network of fine veins of blue mould. Blue Wensleydale shows fewer, but thicker, veins. Blue Vinney is made from skim milk and is so brittle and friable that the 'crumbs' are densely covered with mould.

The manufacture of full-sized blue veined cheese is not advised for the small farm cheese-maker, unless he has some knowledge, and special facilities for ripening. It is possible to make 'Baby Stiltons' if damp ripening premises are available. Small sized cheeses tend to dry out too much for mould development. Semi-hard cheeses made on the Wensleydale principle may also go blue quite satisfactorily. Blue Vinney can be made with simple equipment, but skim milk, not separated milk, must be used, as the cheese requires some amount of fat.

All blue veined cheese requires fat to give much of the characteristic flavour produced by the mould-ripening, so that milk for Stilton cheese is usually fortified by added cream.

Cheese which is required to go blue will often fail to do so, owing to some factor being incorrect. Conversely, cheese which is not meant to grow interior moulds will sometimes develop them. This can occur in semi-hard cheese which is too moist and open textured, and though theoretically a defect, it can be quite a pleasant one. It is amazing how many fallacies exist in the public mind regarding 'blue' cheese. People will devour Blue Stilton, but throw away a piece of blue-moulded Cheddar. Others will swear that the veins are due to the verdigris from copper wires, whereas the 'lines' of mould are simply due to their growth along the piercing. This piercing or 'pricking' is purposely done to let in air to encourage the mould, and copper wires are not used. Another common error is the idea that good Blue Cheese must be 'maggoty', 'mitey', or both. The presence of maggots simply means that the cheese has been blown by flies, and does not necessarily show the cheese to be a good one. Any cheese, at any age, can be attacked by fly. Mites are seen on old cheese, especially Stilton, as a fine dun-coloured dust. They may also appear on any cheese if it is stored for long periods. They belong to a group of spider-like insects which can cause great damage to foodstuffs, and certain varieties find rough-coated cheese an easy prey. The supposition that maggots and mites denote a cheese of good quality has probably arisen because ripe mellow-flavoured cheese may have been attacked during its prolonged ripening.

Group 4: **Soft cheese** Many types. Rennet curds.

Group 5: **Acid-curd cheese** Many types. Made from acid-curds. Full-cream milk, skim milk, or mixtures of them.

The acid-coagulated curds are all suitable for home-manufacture, and are especially useful when only small quantities of milk are available. They do not store, but deteriorate rapidly within a few days of making, so should be consumed, or sold, as fresh as possible.

Group 6: **Cream 'cheese'**

Double cream. Made from 60% ('thick') cream.
Single cream. Made from 30% cream.

The cream 'cheeses' are not made from any basic curd, either acid- or rennet-coagulated. A small amount of rennet may be used as a 'thickening agent' for the single cream. Cream cheese is composed of all constituents of cream, with fat in excess. This is drained of moisture, and subsequently salted. The cream can be sweet or acid, the products being in no way cheese.

Group 7: **'Processed' cheese, and 'Processed cheese spreads'** Processed cheese preparations are not feasible for the small scale manufacturer, as special machinery is required. This is necessary for the actual processing and also for the safety of the product. The cheese purchaser is often confused over the meaning of 'processed' as opposed to 'raw' cheese, and many people have no idea what in fact they are

buying. The public has become increasingly inclined to purchase a product which is known to keep indefinitely if unopened. It has no wastage from rind, possesses unique spreading properties, and has a mild characteristic flavour. The consumer gains these advantages, and pays a higher price to repay the processer for the treatment and packaging. The flavour and texture of the initial raw cheese is entirely changed by the processing, and this is a loss to the consumer, though seldom realised. Processed cheese and Processed cheese spreads are prepared from one or more varieties of cheese, the mix being heat-treated with an emulsifying salt to prevent separation of the fat and protein. The hot mix is packaged direct, 'positively' sealed by machine, and solidified by cooling in its sealed wrapping.

Processed cheese is sufficiently firm to cut, though not too hard to spread, and is sold in blocks as well as small portions. Processed cheese spreads contain a higher content of water, from 48-60% as compared with 42-48% in the firmer type. The spreads remain soft at ordinary temperatures, and often contain curds and other milk products in addition to cheese. The public should realise that the prefix cheese to a spread means that it contains products of 'dairy origin' only. If any substance of non-dairy origin is used, the processed product is a spread, but may bear any proprietary name. All processed products lend themselves to a variety of packs, familiar to the shopping public.

Unprocessed cheese spreads are sometimes marketed, but are usually made up in the form of 'fancy cheese'. These must only contain milk products if the prefix cheese is used. This type of spread has no long keeping properties, as it is not heat treated to destroy micro-organisms. A variety of unprocessed spreads, of milk products or mixtures, can be made in the house for quick consumption.

Nutritional aspects

The nutritional value of cheese and curd products is of great importance. They form one of the chief sources of animal protein, with body-building properties equal to those of lean meat. Cheese does not in fact possess the indigestible qualities so often assigned to it, for the protein is in an easily assimilated form. Digestibility is increased if the protein is mechanically broken, as by grating, or macerating, before consumption.

It is now realised that quite young children benefit by the addition of cheese to their diet. As well as the basic protein, there are valuable mineral constituents, including calcium for bone structure. The fat content varies with the type of cheese. The minimum fat content to be contained in Cheddar Cheese is 48% milk fat in the dry matter, and a maximum of 39% water calculated on the total weight of the cheese.* Cheeses with a higher moisture content, such as the soft varieties, are proportionately lower in protein and fatty solids. They are especially well suited for consumption by children and invalids, who may find the pressed types too strong.

*See Cheese Regulations 1970 Schedule 1, which also details the composition of many other varieties.

Many of these high-moisture curds and cheeses are easily made in the home. Their maximum value and palatability is obtained when eaten fresh. They are not suitable for cooking, though some of the curds can be toasted on bread. The semi-hard cheeses come between the hard-pressed and soft cheese, with an average water content of 37-40%, the protein and fat being proportional. These cheeses have the longest storage properties of all the types which can be made on a small scale. It is possible to ripen them to some extent, but the flavour is not very strong or 'cheesy', and is not sufficiently defined to remain after cooking.

Analysis tables give some indication of the distribution of the milk constituents in the products, and by-products, of manufacture. The term by-product covers skim-milk, separated milk, whey, and buttermilk. All compositions are subject to variation, so the figures quoted below are approximate. They suffice to show which constituents are of major importance to different products, and how they are available for nutritional purposes. Methods of use are dealt with in subsequent chapters.

Colostrum (Beestings) This is so constituted that it forms an ideal food for the new-born animal, being high in albuminous proteins and salts. During the first week of lactation, there is a gradual change in constituents to a normal milk balance.

Colostrum should not be used for butter or cheese-making purposes, as the high albuminous content causes rapid spoilage. These albuminous proteins, albumen and globulin, are the most easily assimilated by the animal. Consequently they are very susceptible to decomposition, as they undergo 'protein digestion' by micro-organisms. They are coagulated by heating to a temperature of 180°F.* or over; hence it is possible to use colostrum as 'beestings pudding'. Colostrum is dark yellow in colour, and salty to taste.

Average percentage composition of milks

Cow's milk immediately after parturition

Water + minerals..... 76.12	Total solids	
Albumen and globulin 11.35	23.88	
Casein 5.08	exclusive	
Lactose.............. 2.19	of	
Fat................. 5.10	nonchloride	
Chloride salts 0.16	salts	

At 7 days after parturition

Water + minerals..... 88.37	Total solids
Albumen and globulin 0.69	11.63
Casein 2.42	exclusive
Lactose............. 4.96	of
Fat................. 3.45	nonchloride
Chloride salts 0.11	salts

Goat's milk The average composition differs from that of normal cow's milk, the total solids content being higher.

Water 84.86	
Albumen and globulin 0.70	
Casein 3.30	Total solids
Lactose............. 4.30	15.14
Fat................. 6.00	
Mineral salts 0.84	

* For Fahrenheit/Centigrade conversion table see page 96.

The high solid content makes it especially nutritious, both for liquid consumption and for product manufacture.

Goats are immune from tuberculosis, so the milk is free from animal infection by the causative organism.

Goat's milk is used extensively in many countries, especially along the Mediterranean coast. In some mountainous and remote areas goats are numerous, and the local population depends on the milk for liquid consumption, butter and cheese. A number of local cheeses are made from both goat's and ewe's milk. These cheeses have characteristic ripening properties and flavour, and are preferred to those made from cow's milk in some countries.

Ewe's milk is even higher in solids, an average % composition being:

Water 76.6	
Albumen and globulin 1.1	
Casein 4.6	Total solids
Lactose............. 4.7	20.4
Fat................. 9.0	
Mineral salts 1.0	

Ewe's milk is not used in Britain, but a considerable amount of goat's milk is produced. The goat population is rather fluctuating, being influenced by current economy, and always increases during periods of emergency and food shortage. A constant number is kept by small farmers and country householders, who find the goat an economic unit with a milk yield of 3-4 pints a day. The 'goaty' flavour should not be apparent in fresh milk, provided the animal is well kept and housed, and the milking done under hygienic conditions. The flavour does develop some hours after it is drawn; this is due to certain natural acids in the milk, and the characteristic flavour and smell become more pronounced as milk gets older, because of the increase in acidity. It is therefore essential to use absolutely fresh milk when making butter or cheese from goat's milk.

The milk constituents are distributed in the various products, but in varying amounts according to type and variety of each. General distribution in cheese-making is as follows:

Milk + Rennet = Curd + Whey
Milk + Lactic Acid ('Souring') = Curd + Whey

In both cases the curd is formed by the coagulation of the casein, and most of the fat and minerals are contained in it. The rennet curd is of completely different protein construction to the acid-curd, so that once milk has been curdled by acidity, it can no longer be acted on by rennet. In both cases the casein is chemically changed during coagulation, as are some of the minerals incorporated in it. The milk fat, which is in the form of globules of varying size, is not affected chemically by the action of rennet or acid. The globules are merely 'held' in the curd, and so can easily be lost by any rough handling. Undue stirring of the milk may cause the fat to churn out, and rough treatment of the curd during cheese manufacture may cause the globules to escape into the whey.

Approximate percentage compositions of types of cheese.

'Green' cheese denotes new, unripe cheese.

Hard pressed cheese

green   Water 37.33
Casein, lactose
and minerals . . . 29.26
Fat 33.41

ripe   Water 33.8
Casein, lactose
and minerals 30.8
Fat 35.4

Semi-hard cheese (green)

Water 37.79
Casein, lactose
and minerals . . . 29.59
Fat 33.62

Soft cheese (green)

Water 51.5
Protein, lactose,
minerals, etc. 21.4
Fat 27.1

These proportions are subject to considerable variations according to the variety of cheese in each group, age of cheese, and composition of initial milk.

Whey

Whey is the greenish liquid which exudes from the curd, and it contains the albumen and globulin, some of the mineral matter, and the milk sugar in solution. Some whey is retained as the moisture content in all cheese, but the lactose dissolved in it rapidly changes to lactic acid. The standard method on the farm is to utilise whey for pig feeding; but when only very small amounts are available from home cheese manufacture, it can be used in several ways. Whey rapidly becomes acid, which means that the sugar, a most valuable nutritional factor, is being lost. To prevent this souring, the whey can be heated to destroy the acid-producing organisms. The heating temperature must not be too high, or the albumen will curdle, so it is safest to use a pasteurising temperature of 160°F. 'Whey cheese' is made by coagulating this albuminous protein, the whey being boiled, and the curd filtered out. Liquid whey can be used in various ways as a beverage. Its usefulness as an invalid drink, or in 'modified' milk for delicate infants, has long been recognised. 'Whey butter' is churned from the cream separated out from whey. Approximately 0.3% fat is left in the whey, so that cream and butter production from it is only economic on a big scale.

Average percentage composition of whey

Water 93.95
Fat 0.30
Albumen and globulin 0.75
Lactose 5.00

Skim milk and separated milk

'Machine skimmed' means the same as separated, i.e. milk from which the fat has been removed mechanically by centrifugal force. The term 'skim' milk means milk from which the fat has been skimmed off by hand, after it has risen as cream to the milk surface. Skim milk is higher in fat than separated milk, the amount varying with the efficiency of skimming. Both are extremely valuable protein foods, and should be utilised whenever possible. The average person is liable to assess milk from its fat content only, and this is a grave nutritional error. Most of the separated and skim milk on farms is fed to stock and poultry, but it would be advisable to use more in the home.

Percentage composition of separated milk

Water 90.90
Fat 0.05
Casein 2.65
Albumen and globulin 0.77
Lactose 4.93
Minerals 0.70

Efficiently machine-separated milk will not contain more than 0.05% fat but hand-skimmed milk may contain 0.7%.

Buttermilk

This is the by-product from churning cream into butter. When undiluted, it has approximately the same composition as skim milk, and should be utilised whenever possible. The flavour will vary according to whether sweet or acid cream has been churned. The lactose content will be reduced in the acid type.

2 CHEESEMAKING IN FARM AND HOME

Whoever decides to make cheese must first consider where he or she can make it. The choice must obviously depend on the facilities available, and though there is often plenty of scope in the farmhouse, the ordinary house-holder may not be so fortunate. Here the kitchen and scullery may be the only available rooms, and cheese-making must be fitted in with routine housework. There is a tendency for high or fluctuating temperatures, according to

the type of cooking stove installed, and space is often limited. The farmer's wife can usually adapt a larder or storeroom where she will find old slate slabs a useful place for cheese drainage. A utility area, or similar type of room, can also be used, and it is an added advantage if hot and cold water are available.

Whatever place is chosen, the floor should be of stone, cement, tile or brick, as there may be considerable splashing of water and whey. It is best if there is floor drainage, but if this is not present, water can be mopped up. Wood floors are inadvisable, as they are difficult to clean, and easily become contaminated with milk or whey. No soft coverings should be on the floor, and the old practice of draining moisture on to sacks is a bad one, as they become very foul, and are difficult to clean. The question of hygiene is extremely important, as milk and milk products can be ruined if contaminated from dirty surroundings.

Temperature control can also affect both manufacture and storage of cheese. The range 50°–60°F. is a safe one, but often the making rooms tend to be too high, and storage rooms such as cellars, too low, in temperature. Rooms also vary in suitability according to weather, and may be too hot and dry in the summer, and too cold and humid in winter. Ventilation must be efficient, but direct draughts are bad. Considerable space is required to allow for easy handling, depending on the quantity of milk being used, and the type of manufacture. Sufficient space for drainage of several days' make of cheese is necessary, for which tables, benches, trestles and planks, or wall shelving, are all suitable. If the cheese requires storage for several weeks, it is best removed from the making room to an improvised store. Cellars can often be adapted for this purpose.

Preparation of the premises chosen is very important, and must be completed before they are used for cheese-making purposes. Unless the cleaning is really efficient, there may be contamination of the milk, which can lead to serious troubles in manufacture, and to defects in the cheese. Special care must be taken with rooms which have been empty for a long period, or those which have been used for farm stores. The ceiling, walls, floor, and any shelving must first be brushed thoroughly, to remove dirt, dust, cobwebs and dead insects. Dry brushing should be followed by hot water cleansing of all surfaces. Ceiling and walls should be washed down by spraying all over from a stirrup-pump, or hand farm-sprayer. The floor should be swilled and brushed down. All shelving, tables and benches must be thoroughly scrubbed with hot water and soda or detergent. As a final precaution, all surfaces can be sprayed, or wiped over, with a dilute solution of hypochlorite, approximately one egg-cupful to three gallons of water.

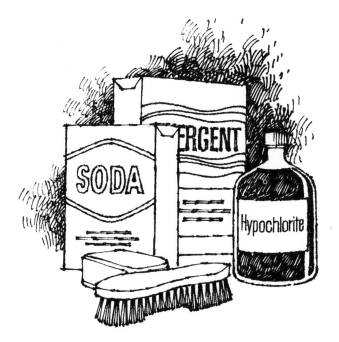

Before any form of sterilisation is used, it is essential to thoroughly clean all utensils. First rinse off all traces of milk or curd with *cold* water. Hot water will harden some protein constituents on to the surfaces. Scrub thoroughly in hot water, using a detergent to remove grease and any hardened scum. Brush all surfaces thoroughly with a stiff brush but do not scratch metal surfaces with pan cleaners. Rinse off detergent, and sterilise. If a chest is available, invert utensils and steam at 210°F. for 20-30 minutes. Alternatively, dip the cleaned utensils in boiling water, and leave them inverted in a clean place to dry off. If using hypochlorite solution, dip the previously cleaned utensil in the solution, then wash off all traces of the hypochlorite in hot water, and invert until required for use. Be absolutely certain that all grease and milk scum is removed *before* using the hypochlorite, as its sterilising action is prevented unless surfaces are absolutely clean.

Apparatus and equipment required

Items essential for all types of milk product manufacture

Glass measure Capacity 4 fluid oz. (32 fluid drachms). Graduated in drachms and ounces.

Glass measure Capacity 1 drachm (or 60 minims). Graduated in minims.

Graduated measures are absolutely necessary for accurate work, and are well worth the small cost. They are obtainable at dairy supply stores, chemists, and photographic stores.

Floating (Dairy) *thermometers* graduated to 212° Fahrenheit scale*.

*See Conversion Table page 96

Cleaning of equipment

The same rules apply to all the equipment used for cheese-making. Cleaning and sterilisation should be carried out each time after use, so that the milk will not be contaminated by any surface with which it comes in contact. Where no steriliser is available, hypochlorite-sterilisation can be practised. If there are facilities for heating up large quantities of water, dipping of cleaned utensils in water at boiling point can be quite effective.

Wall thermometers to check atmospheric temperature in making and storage rooms are optional, but useful.

Thermometers are required for checking the temperature of all liquids during treatment or manufacture of milk products. They are obtainable at dairy supply stores, and are so constructed that they will float upright in the liquid. Mercury-filled stems are preferable to alcohol. The latter are easier to read, but if the coloured liquid escapes from an accidentally broken thermometer, the milk or cream is spoilt. If a mercury type thermometer is broken, the broken glass and mercury can be seived out by pouring the milk or cream through a muslin stretched over a container, without adverse effect. Of course, the presence of broken glass, mercury, or any foreign body is illegal in any food product offered for sale. Its finding by any member of the public can lead to legal proceedings being taken against the maker of the product.

Additional items required for all types of small scale cheese-making

Containers for holding the milk. Type, and size will obviously depend on the amount of milk being handled, and the outlay considered economic.

The orthodox type of vat, or tub, is constructed of tinned steel (stainless steel is extremely costly). It may be circular, or rectangular, and have outer jackets for holding hot water. The less expensive ones are not jacketed, but all should have handles for lifting. Their capacities vary from 10-20 gallons. Metal containers are easier to clean and sterilise, and will stand up to many years of service.

Wooden tubs are cheaper, and if kept in good condition will stand up to hard wear. They are more difficult to clean effectively and sterilise, and are liable to contamination, especially by yeasts and moulds. Soaking in water is necessary during long periods when the tub is not in use. This is to prevent the staves from separating, when contraction of the wood allows the enclosing metal band to slip. The wood swells up again when soaked, and the band and staves can be replaced.

If wooden tubs have previously been used for other purposes, especially any concerned with fermentations, they must be cleaned thoroughly with detergent, and subsequently steamed (or heated with boiling water) before being used for milk. If any metal container is substituted for an orthodox type, it is essential that it is free from rust, and has sufficiently smooth surfaces to clean easily. It must be of metal which does not corrode with the action of acid—preferably with a tinned surface. Tinned steel and aluminium alloys are suitable. Galvanised iron and zinc must never be used.

Plastic buckets and bins of all sizes are now in common use, and have the advantage of being cheap to buy and easy to clean.

Buckets of 2-3 gallons capacity are suitable for all small scale work. They must be of good quality, preferably tinned steel. Stainless steel buckets are very expensive. Buckets of cheap metal must not be used.

Scales and Weights Kitchen or farm scales can be used for weighing finished curd, according to the amount. Weights are used for 'dead-weight' pressing of curd in the moulds, when no orthodox cheese press is available. Sizes required are from one pound to fourteen pounds, and any spare weights available can be cleaned and painted for use, as they need not be completely accurate. These weights do not actually touch the curd, but it is nevertheless important to keep them free from rust, as it may flake off on to the cheese.

Cloths for Cheese-making Several types and weaves of cloth are needed. These can be bought as yardage from dairy supply stores, which is the cheapest method. If only a few yards are required, substitutes for the dairy cloths can be bought at most stores. Those required are:

Coarse Weave Linen (Scrim) Used when making semi-hard cheese.

Fine Weave Linen and Huckaback Used as drainage cloths for soft cheese curds, acid curds, and cream 'cheese'.

'Cheese Grey' Unbleached finely woven cotton material, used for lining moulds and bandaging cheese.

Butter Muslin Used for lining some soft cheese moulds, and for wrapping cream 'cheese'. Also for sieve-cloths and straining cloths.

Linen Thread Used for sewing up cheese bandages.

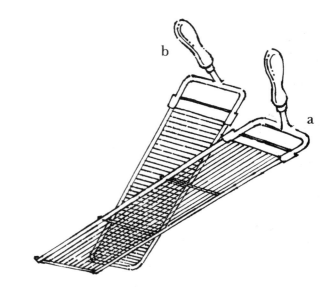

*American curd knives, with vertical blades (**a**) and with horizontal blades (**b**).*

Cutters When fairly large amounts are to be made, it is worth while investing in a pair of cheese knives (American curd knives). One knife should have vertical blades, and the other horizontal, with a spacing between the blades of ¼-½ inch. For small quantities, ordinary knives of 'carver' type can be used. They are best of stainless steel, as the ordinary steel blades are quickly corroded by whey.

Moulds and Hoops These are required for shaping the cheese, under pressure. 'Baby' Cheshire moulds are procurable to make one pound and two pound sized cheese. Size of moulds:

2lb: height 5 inches × 4½ inches diameter
1lb: height 4 inches × 3½ inches diameter

'Loaf' cheese moulds are for 4-10 lb. sizes. This type of mould consists of a perforated metal cylinder, of tinned steel, with a fused base, and fitting metal follower to place on top. One wooden follower is additionally provided for each mould. Caerphilly moulds of orthodox size are of 10 inches diameter × 2½ inches height, and have a fused base. The holding capacity is the amount of curd produced from 7 gallons of milk. This type of mould does not have any followers, but has a metal hoop or collar which slips down inside. The moulds are filled with the collars extended, and are pressed one above the other. The collars sink as the curd is consolidated, and the base of the mould above acts in place of a follower. If an individual Caerphilly type of cheese is made, a fitting metal plate must be used, on top of the collar on which the weight is placed.

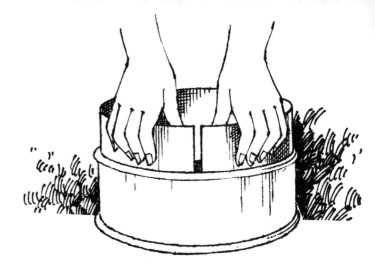

The collar of a Caerphilly mould is a pliable strip of tinned steel which is fitted within the mould and then raised just far enough to stay within the mould. The collar gradually sinks as the curd consolidates under pressure.

A perforated 'loaf' cheese mould, with its metal and wooden followers.

Ordinary cake tins provide efficient substitutes for moulds, especially the flat ones required for the Farm Pressed, White Wensleydale, and allied varieties. The best type to use are those in the form of a metal hoop, with a separate fitting metal plate. The hoop is stood on a board, the curd filled in, and the plate fitted on top to take the weight. The metal used for cake-tins is thin, so easily buckles unless the weight is evenly distributed. Buckling can be prevented by inserting a tin or enamel dish between the metal plate and the weight. The term 'hoop' is used for any curd container that does not have a fused base, and is suitable for cheeses which receive little or no pressure. They are not satisfactory if the curd requires much pressure, as it squeezes through beneath the open hoop.

Additional apparatus for soft cheese-making

Scoops and Ladles These can be bought quite cheaply, in aluminium alloy, and are similar to those in general kitchen use. Large-sized metal spoons are useful, as they can cut thin even slices of curd, and are comparatively inexpensive.

Hoops are required into which the curd is filled for draining and shaping. The Coulommier type is in two parts, one fitting into the other, the flexibility of the metal allowing the two hoops to be pressed into position. The upper hoop is removed when the curd has sunk below its level. There are no perforations. Two sizes are made, the larger to yield two cheeses per gallon of milk, and the smaller three cheeses per gallon of milk. Approximate sizes are:

Large

bottom hoop: height 3 inches × 6 inches diameter

top hoop: height 2¼ inches × 6 inches diameter

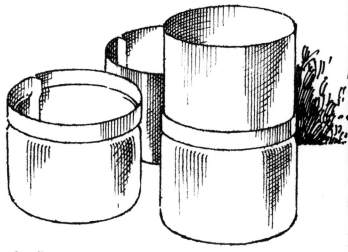

Coulommier hoops, shown separate, and when fitted together.

Small

bottom hoop: height 3 inches × 4¼ inches diameter

top hoop: height 2½ inches × 4½ inches diameter

The orthodox Colwick cheese hoop is a single perforated hoop, approximately 7 inches high × 5 inches diameter. Coulommier hoops may be used instead.

As an emergency measure, ordinary 2 lb. round tins, such as those for cocoa, can be used. The base must be cut out to form a 'hoop'. These tins are for short service only, and require care in handling owing to the sharp ends. The moulds for Cambridge or York cheese cannnot easily be substituted, as they are made in two parts. The top portion, rectangular in shape, is approximately 8 inches long by 5 inches wide by 6 inches deep. It fits into the bottom portion which is in the form of a shallow tray. This holds the fitted straw mat on to which the curd is ladled. These moulds may be constructed of tinned steel, or of wood. The wooden ones are difficult to clean, and less hard-wearing than the metal ones, but have the advantage of keeping the curd warmer by good insulation properties. Additionally, the characteristic appearance of the cheese surface is produced by the curling over of the curd at the corners of wooden moulds.

Wooden boards are required on which to place the straw mats and hoops. Also for turning the cheese during drainage. They are 12 inches long by 8 inches wide by ½ inch thick, and must be made of hard, well-seasoned wood, free from aroma.

The straw mats were originally made by threading together rye straws. They are now procurable, ready for use, composed of shaped wood pulp. They are of the same size as the boards, and must be carefully cleaned, boiled, and dried off. Otherwise they rapidly deteriorate,

and become a source of contamination.

Choice of milk for cheese-making

The fermentations which occur during the manufacture and subsequent ripening of cheese depend on the action of micro-organisms in the milk. The type of organisms present affects the process of manufacture, and the flavour and quality of the cheese. The 'souring' organisms in milk are essential, but the amount must not be excessive as too much acidity is then formed. Organisms which produce tainted flavours and gas have an adverse effect, and must be prevented by hygienic milk production and constant care in the cleaning and sterilisation of all milk and cheese equipment. Usually it is the surplus milk on a farm which is available for cheese-making. This may mean good quality milk, retained for the purpose, but more often it is 'Rejected' milk or dairy 'Returns'. Rejected milk has been refused by the depot or dairy, because it has failed to pass the reception tests for hygienic quality, and is sometimes returned to the farm that has produced it. Returns usually denote unsold bulk, or bottled milks, which may be in good, or bad, condition according to the time and conditions of storage. Care is therefore required in deciding whether surplus milks are suitable for use, and if so, for what purpose.

It is safe to use returns if not more than 24 hours of age, and if intervening storage has been at a low temperature. If the milk has become acid, it can most economically be used to make acid-curd types of cheese, provided the acidity is clean. The term 'clean acidity' denotes one which possesses a pleasantly acid taste and smell, free from bad flavours or taints.

The decision on rejected milk depends on the cause for its refusal. If refused because of acidity, it may be used for acid-curds; or, if only slightly acid, for other types of cheese. If it is tainted badly, or shows broken flakes of cream on the surface when the milk churn* is opened, it is unsuitable, as it may contaminate utensils and spoil the cheese. Such milk is best fed to stock.

The best plan is to retain some of the milk on the farm, choosing the most suitable supply for cheese-making purposes. Such milk should be full-cream, hygienically produced, and stored or handled in sterilised apparatus.

To obtain a better fat balance in the milk for semi-hard and soft cheese, approximately half the required amount should be retained from the richer evening milk, to be mixed later with the morning's milk of the next day. The retained evening milk must be carefully stored overnight. If retained for soft cheese, it should be cooled to cold water temperature to check development of acidity, and kept as cool as possible until used. When needed for semi-hard varieties, which require some degree of acidity in the milk, it can be ripened during the overnight storage. The ripening of the evening milk must be varied according to prevailing temperature. If the weather is hot, the milk is better cooled to cold water temperature, and left in the container overnight. No lid should be

* All farm milk has been collected in bulk in Britain since July 1979—churns are no longer used.

placed over the vat, but a piece of cloth to cover it is an advisable protection. If the night temperature is low, then the milk can be left warm in the container. The interval between the milkings allows some of the lactic acid-producing (souring) organisms to become active, and causes a preliminary ripening of the milk.

Care must be taken not to let the milk become too acid, as this spoils manufacture. It is safer to hold a cooled milk, but in this case some ripening period must be allowed after the two lots of milk are mixed the next day. The fat will rise on to the surface of the evening milk, and as it will not always re-mix easily, it is better to skim the fat off into a separate vessel before adding the morning milk. It should be heated to 90° and then re-mixed with the milk in the vat. The whole can then be carefully stirred at intervals until ready for renneting.

Taints in milk

During any period of milk storage, it is essential to keep it removed from any contaminating substances. Taints, or bad flavours, which can be very severe in milk, are of many types. Most are due to the action of undesirable micro-organisms which gain access at the time of milking from unclean utensils, or from any dust or dirt in the air and buildings. This kind of taint is bad for cheese-making, as it may persist throughout manufacture, and even spoil the cheese. If there has been manurial contamination, there may also be production of gas, which will 'blow' the curd by the formation of holes, making it spongy during manufacture. A cheese made from such a curd will usually blow in the storage room, and may also taste unpleasant. This kind of taint is more liable to occur at *higher* temperatures, so especial care is necessary if warm evening milk is kept over. Fortunately with the modern methods of hygienic milk production, the danger of contamination by taint and gas-forming organisms is much reduced.

Certain types of taints are not due to the action of organisms but may be 'derived' or 'absorbed'. Derived types are those which are caused by some substance consumed by the cow, the flavour-producing portion passing through with the milk. Examples of this type are the strong smell and taste of field garlic, tansy, turnip, and silage. Absorbed taints are those which are actually taken up by the milk from some substance near which it is left. Examples are the absorption of taste and smell from creosote, paraffin, paints, or strong smelling foods such as onions. Sometimes it is difficult to distinguish the source of a taint, because some of those produced by micro-organisms are very similar in smell to other types. Examples of this are 'weedy' and 'turnipy' taints which can appear in milk when no such foods have been eaten by the cow, or been near the milk. If a taint persists in milk from the farm, a simple test can be made to prove whether it is caused by micro-organisms, or due to some other cause.

Taint test

1. Fill a pint* bottle with the suspect milk, and cover the top

2. Take a pint bottle of milk obtained from another farm, or from a dairy. Shake the bottle,

then uncap carefully, pour away about two tablespoonsful of the contents.

3. Re-fill up to the top with milk from the suspect bottle, exposing as little to the air as possible.

4. Re-cover, and leave in a warm place for 6-12 hours.

5. Uncap, and smell the contents.

If the bought milk has developed the taint, it is proved to be caused by micro-organisms, which have been transferred, and grown in the new supply. If no taint has developed, the taint is derived, or absorbed, from another source, and is non-transferable.

Having chosen a milk of the best hygienic quality, the cheese-maker must then consider its chemical composition. This must be well-balanced, so that the curd formed will have good draining properties, and retain the fat to give a mellow texture.

The term 'full-cream milk' denotes that from which no fat has been removed, and if cheese is sold as full-cream, it must be made from such milk, with no addition of separated or skim milk. Cheese for home consumption, and varieties containing low fat, may be made from mixtures of full-cream and separated milk as desired by the maker. For full-cream milk cheese, a higher fat content gives a bigger yield of cheese, within limits. If the fat is too high (over 4%) there is wastage by loss of fat into the whey. The fat has a mellowing effect on curd and cheese, and if it is too low (3% or below), the curd produced is hard and the cheese harsh and dry. Hence the advisability of balancing up

* Take at least half a litre.

by judicious mixing of morning and evening milk. The ideal is to obtain a mixture with a sufficiently high content of casein to yield a stable curd, which can 'hold' the fat to yield a mellow cheese.

Heat treatment of milk

The heat-treatment (also referred to as pasteurisation) of milk for cheese-making purposes is practised in large scale manufacture, as the heating destroys many of the micro-organisms, and they are replaced by an inoculation of special cultures of lactic acid-producing organisms. For small scale work, milk of good hygienic quality can safely and most economically be used raw. If it is of doubtful quality, then heat treatment may be worth while; but this should be omitted if possible. It need not require complicated apparatus, but increases the time spent. It is essential to check the heating temperature carefully by means of a thermometer, as if the temperature rises too high some salts in the milk are changed; the action of rennet is thereby reduced or prevented, and the texture of the curd and cheese affected. The best method is to heat up the milk as quickly as possible to a temperature of 150°, and then to cool it down immediately to within the range of 85-95°F. Milk which has been heat treated may not develop acidity, owing to destruction of micro-organisms, so the cheese-maker must use 'starter' when making semi-hard or other types requiring lactic acid production.

The method used for heat-treatment must depend on facilities available in farm or home. Small quantities of milk can be treated in a double saucepan. Larger amounts can be heated by suspending the buckets or containers in a tub of boiling water, stirring the milk while heating. Sufficient hot water may be difficult to obtain, but a farmhouse copper is sometimes available, and can supply hot water for filling other containers, or be itself used for holding the buckets of milk.

Inhibitive substances in milk

The cheese-maker will sometimes find that no development of acidity takes place, and normal procedure is prevented. This is chiefly a problem of large scale manufacture, but individual supplies of farm milk may be affected. It is sometimes due to the presence of antibiotics in the milk, or to contamination with hypochlorite solution. Modern veterinary practice makes valuable use of penicillin and other antibiotics in the treatment of mastitis in cows. Most farmers are now familiar with this form of treatment, but it is not always realised that the action of the lactic acid-producing micro-organisms is inhibited by even minute quantities of milk from an injected udder. Milk from a recently injected cow must never be used for cheese-making, and if the herd has had 'blitz' treatment by universal injection, then the bulk milk must not be used for cheese-making for at least three days afterwards and in some cases much longer.

Hypochlorite solution will also prevent bacterial action, so especial care must be taken to avoid the use of too strong solutions, to prevent any possibility of splashing into the milk, and to rinse off all traces of the solution when it has been used for sterilising equipment.

Substances used in cheese-making

Starter The use of starter is necessary for large scale cheese-making, but as previously explained, it need only be used in small scale production as a means of ensuring the presence of lactic acid-producing organisms. The small-scale maker is advised to use it if the milk is of doubtful hygienic quality, if it has been heat treated at home, or if pasteurised milk has been bought. The starter used for dairy purposes is a growth of special cultures in sterile milk, of the correct strains of those micro-organisms which produce lactic acid fermentation of the lactose or milk sugar. They are prepared in laboratories, and growing cultures, ready for use, can be obtained by the cheese-maker in small bottles.*

The contents of the bottle can be used for direct addition to the cheese-making milk, and starter from one bottle can be used safely for a period of three days, providing it is kept closed and in a cool place, in the intervals between use. One bottle is sufficient for 2-3 gallons of milk. It is expensive constantly to renew supplies, so if

cheese-making is continuing for some time, it is worth while re-cultivating the starter in the following way:

Put two pints of milk into a double saucepan, heat to 210°F. and maintain at that temperature for thirty minutes, checking temperature by means of a floating thermometer which is left in the milk throughout the heating. Then cool the milk to a temperature of 75°F., by placing the pan in cold water. Pour the milk into a container which has previously been well scalded in boiling water (or steam sterilised when a steaming chest is available). Add the contents of the bottle of starter. Stir it in thoroughly and leave container, covered, in a warm room overnight.

Making one's own supply of starter culture. The previously heated and cooled milk is ready for the addition of the bought starter. It will be ready for use the next day.

*Starter cultures are now available in freeze dried or deep frozen form.

34

By the next day the inoculated milk should have curdled, and can then itself be used as a starter. Retain a portion of this for repeating the process each day. By this means a new supply is made daily, and can be safely used for as long as it retains its purity and activity. This will depend on the care taken in the daily cultivation, but if in good condition, the curd formed each day will be firm and acid, smell clean, and have a sharp acid taste. Before using, the curd must be stirred to break it up, so that it can be poured into a measure, for adding to the cheese-making milk.

Starter should be renewed from source if and when the one 'carried over' shows signs of contamination, or of weakening. Weakening is shown by slow acid production, the curd formed after 12 hours remaining soft. Contamination is proved by the smell being cheesy, yeasty, or otherwise tainted. The curd may also be flaky, with whey around the particles, or it may be holey, from gas formation. Moulds may be seen growing on the surface of the curd, showing as velvety white or greenish patches. It is unwise to continue using starter if it shows any of these effects, as it may contaminate the cheese.

Starter can also be used for souring cream for butter-making, and for making acid-curds. Surplus starter can be used direct for the latter, or milk may be curdled by starter and the curd used. It is the safest way of preventing defects of flavour, which are often evident in milk curds soured without starter.

'Natural' starter If it is considered too expensive to buy bottles of starter culture, natural starter can be used instead. This can be a dangerous source of trouble in the products, as its purity depends on the initial state of the milk used for the purpose. Milk used must therefore be of the highest standard in hygienic quality, to give a souring agent which is safe.

Choose the milk from a healthy cow, being certain that the fore-milk has been rejected. Take all precautions to ensure absolute cleanliness during milking. Pour the milk, at blood heat as drawn, into a previously sterilised container. Do not heat-treat, as in this case the natural lactic organisms must not be destroyed. Leave the covered container in a warm place until curdling has occurred. A firm solid curd should be formed within 24-48 hours. This curd is safe to use as starter if it is solid, and cleanly acid in taste and smell. If carried over by inoculation, as previously described, it is liable to deteriorate more quickly than when the first inoculation is made from a prepared culture. This is because other micro-organisms from the milk may be present in the natural starter, and these may outgrow the lactic acid-producing ones. Signs of contamination may therefore appear more quickly.

Rennet is an extract, in brine, of one of the digestive juices occurring in the stomach of mammals. It has the specific property of coagulating milk, and has additionally some protein-digestive action. Its primary use in cheese-making is to act on the casein in the milk, which is 'thrown down' as a solid coagulum, to form the basic curd of the cheese. It also influences the ripening, because the vital factor of the extract (the enzyme rennin) continues to act on the protein, though not to so obvious an extent as the micro-organisms.

The amount and quality of the rennet extract used can consequently affect the type of curd formed, and its ripening properties of flavour and texture production. The activity of rennet on milk is increased with rises in temperature and acidity, and decreased when milk has been heat-treated, is very 'sweet', or is at a low temperature. The temperature range used for adding rennet to milk for cheese-making is from 85-95°F, which results in a firm curd, sufficiently strong to hold the fat, and handle easily during manufacture. If the temperature when adding rennet is too high, or if too much extract is used, the curd formed is too hard. It contracts and dries out, resulting in a harsh cheese with dry chalky texture.

Rennet was at one time prepared on the farm, being known as runnet, a term often used in old books. Runnet was obtained from the vells (or stomachs) of suckling calves, as the secretion of the specific digestive juice is greatest while milk is being ingested. The vells were removed at slaughter, and could be used direct, or stored after a rough drying by suspension in a cool place. Subsequently the vells were cut up, and crushed and soaked in tubs of brine for several weeks. The vital coagulating factor exuded into the brine, and the liquid was crudely filtered, and stored in wooden or earthenware containers. The actual vell could also be used as.a coagulant, by adding a cut portion to the milk. This saved the trouble of brine extraction, but was less certain in its effect on the milk. Both methods are still used in some countries, where home-made rennet is preferred for the manufacture of certain varieties of cheese, as it gives a soft curd, and contains micro-organisms which help the specific ripening. In Great Britain the rennet made in this way is very variable in its strength, and owing to the inevitable contamination occurring during its making, it contains many micro-organisms which are not suitable for the lactic-acid type of ripening.

Standard Cheese-making Rennet Extract is prepared commercially and can easily be obtained. The extraction method is in principle the same as for runnet, but sterilisation of equipment, control of extractions, and hygienic care during manufacture and filtering, guarantee a product which is safe to use. It is also of standard strength, so can be measured accurately. It is put up in glass or plastic containers of varying size, and any container used must exclude light, as its action weakens the strength of the extract.

Certain precautions should be taken in the handling and care of rennet, and the following points are worth noting.

Buy in small quantities only, as old rennet is not safe; it gradually loses strength, and inevitably becomes contaminated. Keep the container well corked, and re-cork immediately after use. Do not shake the container, as incorporated air weakens the extract. Do not let any milk splash into the rennet jar, and never dip a dirty spoon, or measure, into it. Always pour rennet from the container into the measuring jar, and do not measure out until just before use. Store the container in a cool place. Note the appearance and smell of the rennet at intervals, and discard it if it looks cloudy, or smells putrid. Liquid rennet is correctly a clear amber-brown, with a peculiar and characteristic smell.

Junket rennet This is not suitable for cheese-making, being approximately six times weaker. Cheese-making rennet can be used for junket making, provided it is diluted six times its volume before being measured for use. The same rules apply to junket rennet as to cheese rennet, the most important point being to purchase small amounts, and to renew frequently.

All rennets are less active on milk which has been heat-treated, therefore the amounts used must be increased by one quarter when making cheese from heated milk, and when making junket from bottled pasteurised milk.

Vegetable rennet Some plants contain enzymes which will coagulate milk; these have been used in many Eastern countries, and references to their use appear in old British books. The British plants chiefly named for the purpose are ladies' bedstraw and butterwort. The use of plant remains is not practicable, as their action is fluctuating, and their effect on the cheese uncertain. Standardised Vegetable and Microbial Rennet is now on the market.

Annatto This is the colouring matter used for cheese and butter, which is added to the milk, or cream. It is a vegetable dye, the pigments being extracted from the seeds of a tropical plant (*Bixa orellana*). There are two distinct types of annatto on the market, one prepared for use in cheese milk, and the other for colouring cream for butter making. The pigments for cheese milk are extracted by alkaline solutions, and the colour is taken up by the protein constituents, remaining in the curd with little loss in the whey. Acid protein will not absorb the pigment, so annatto must not be added to curdled milk. Annatto for butter making purposes is an extract in refined vegetable oil, the colour being transmitted to the fat. It cannot be used for colouring cheese milk, as the oily solution floats on the top, and no colour is absorbed. Cheese annatto can be used for butter, but it is not so satisfactory, there being less transmission of colour to the fat than with the type prepared in oil. The advantages of annatto are its completely non-toxic properties, and if of good quality, there can be no adverse effects on flavour. Its use is entirely optional, but the home cheese maker may find it an added attraction to the cheese, and useful for deepening butter colour at times of year when it is naturally pale, or when the cream is produced from goat's milk.

The 'red' cheeses such as some Cheshire, and Leicester, are coloured with annatto, and the sales value of the baby semi-hard cheese of the Cheshire type can be increased in areas where coloured cheese is in demand. It can also be used for colouring an intermediate portion of soft cheese curd, forming a so-called 'Cream Slice', and for giving a creamier colour to pale acid-curds. The use of annatto to colour milk or cream for sale is prohibited by law.

Precautions in the handling of annatto extracts As in the case of rennet, avoid all possibilities of contamination. Buy small quantities, as it deteriorates with storage. Store in a cool place in light-proof containers. Discard if the smell becomes unpleasant, or if sediment forms. The latter shows as small orange-red specks, which do not dissolve, but float in the milk. They become incorporated in the curd, and cause defective spots of colour in the cheese.

Salt Common salt (sodium chloride) is added to curd as a flavouring and preserving agent. It is also required for making a soakage brine for some varieties of cheese. Household block salt can be used quite satisfactorily, though the crystals are rather tough to mix easily into curd. Specially prepared dairy substances, of finer crystals and guaranteed purity from chemical substances can be obtained in bulk. This type is advisable if sufficient cheese is made or brine required to justify the purchase of salt by the sack. Otherwise block salt can be used, provided it is broken up finely before mixing. When brine is required, block salt may be rather costly, as it takes twenty pounds of salt in 8 gallons of water to make 10 gallons of brine of the correct strength. This brine can be used for a considerable time, provided it is kept in a porcelain sink, or non-corrosive container. The brine needs to be discarded when the smell becomes unpleasant, excess surface scum is formed, or if the cheese becomes slimy on the surface after soakage.

Salt for use in a dairy should be stored in a dry place, as damp causes the salt to harden into rocks which are very difficult to break up. Put sacks of salt on a wooden platform, never directly on to stone or brick floors. Pack block salt in a dry cupboard, keeping paper covering intact. If stored loose, keep all salt in a covered wooden container. Any metal in contact with salt will quickly corrode, and discolour the salt. Keep all sodium chloride apart from other salts and detergents used in farm or dairy. Dangerous confusion can result if calcium chloride (used for refrigerant brine), or if any of the white crystalline powders and salts used for cleaning purposes, are stored in the same place as dairy salt.

Weights and measures used: *
1 gallon water weighs 10 lb.
1 gallon milk weighs approximately 10.32 lb.
1 gallon is the equivalent of:

> 4 quarts
> 8 pints
> 32 gills
> 1 gill = 5 oz.

* See also conversion tables on page 96

38

3 MAKING SEMI-HARD CHEESE

Sequence of processes:

Preparation and ripening of the milk
Addition of colour and rennet
Cutting the curd
Stirring and cooking (scalding) of curd
Drawing the whey
Handling the curd in vat or tub
Salting the curd
Moulding the curd
Pressing the cheese
Ripening and storage of the cheese

For small-scale work, methods must be reduced to the simplest; they must nevertheless conform to the fundamental principles involved. The actual methods of handling can then be modified to any specific type or variety of cheese.

Preparation and ripening of milk

All milk must be strained into the container, through a clean muslin cloth. Ripening denotes the development of lactic acidity, which is not required to any great amount in the semi-hard cheese. As previously explained, sufficient acidity can usually be attained by holding the evening's milk overnight, in the proportion of half the volume to be handled, and mixing in the same amount of morning's milk the following day. If the weather is warm, or the room temperature 60°F. or over, sufficient acidity develops in the evening's milk, and the mixed milk will probably be ready for renneting after one hour of holding the mixture at 85°F. When starter is used, this is added to the mixed milk, and less time (30-40 minutes) allowed for the acidity to develop.

It is difficult to estimate degrees of acidity, and until some experience is gained by taste and smell, time and temperature must be the guiding factors. If a considerable amount of semi-hard cheese-making is contemplated, it may be worth while to buy an acidimeter. This can be used for testing acidity throughout the cheese-making process, and is quite simple to operate. It is known as Lloyd's caustic soda test, and can be bought as an assembled unit, complete with required chemicals and glass-ware. It can be used for testing cream as well as for milk and whey.

The test gives the approximate percentage degree of acidity present in the tested liquid, the degree being calculated from the amount of alkaline caustic soda required to neutralise the acid in a known amount of liquid. The acidity of fresh milk will read between 0.15% and 0.17%, and when sufficiently ripe for semi-hard cheese, it may have risen to 0.18 - 0.19%.

The testing apparatus consists of a glass burette, graduated in millilitres. The burette is filled with a solution of caustic soda of special strength (ninth normal), which can be released slowly by means of a small tap. The burette is supported on a stand, and can be refilled as required with caustic soda solution. A bottle of 'indicator' is also supplied, as this is required to show the point at which neutralisation has occurred. The indicator used is phenol-phthalein, which has the property of being colourless in acid liquids, and pink in alkaline.

Method of taking Lloyd's caustic soda test Suck up the liquid to be tested in a glass pipette, to the point marked '10 mls'. Release into the white porcelain dish provided, and add 1 ml. of phenolphthalein. Adjust the caustic soda level in the burette to the 0 mark, to make reading easier (though when practised, any noted level may be used). Run caustic soda into the liquid in the porcelain vessel—do this very slowly and stir all the time. Continue until the liquid turns very faintly pink. Note the level on the burette containing the caustic soda, and calculate the number of millilitres from 0 that have been needed. For example, if 1.6mls have been used, shown by one large division and six small ones, the relative acidity is 0.16%, as the final result is given by simply moving the decimal point one place to the left.

Degree of ripening of milk, and therefore relative acidity, can also be calculated by a simple rennet test, requiring no complicated apparatus. It depends on the number of seconds required to coagulate a known amount

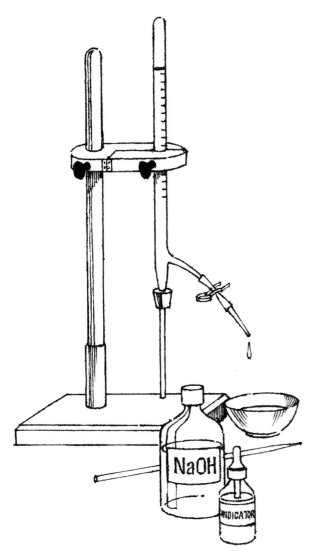

If you plan to make considerable quantities of semi-hard cheese, then apparatus for testing the milk's acidity and its readiness for renneting, may be helpful. Caustic soda solution is carefully added to the milk and indicator in the dish. When the acid in the milk is neutralized by the caustic soda, its colour will change, and the degree of acidity can be simply calculated from the amount of alkali used.

of milk. The drachm and fluid ounce measures can be used from the cheese equipment—the only extra item is a clock or watch with a dial reading in seconds.

Method of rennet test Measure out 4 oz. of milk, and place the glass in warm water. Adjust the temperature to 87°F., and keep as near to this temperature as possible. Measure 1 dm standard cheese rennet, and pour into a cup. Float some pieces of cut straw, or match ends, on top of the rennet. Note the time on the watch, and pour milk at 87° on to rennet. Stir renneted milk to keep straws moving, for 15 seconds, using the thermometer as stirrer. Note temperature on withdrawing. Watch milk and rennet carefully, and immediately straws stop moving, note the exact time on watch, as this is the point at which coagulation has occurred. Calculate the total number of seconds taken from adding milk to rennet, to when the straws stop moving. The critical temperature is 85°F., and if milk is poured in at 87°, it will usually have fallen to 85° after the 15 seconds' stirring. If not at 85°, subtract 2 seconds from the reading for every degree of temperature below 85°, and add 2 for any one degree above, because the action of rennet is hastened by higher temperature, and vice versa. For example, if the number of seconds taken is 25, at a temperature of 83°, the true reading is 21, as the lower temperature has slowed up the rennet action by 4 seconds. If the number of seconds taken is 25, at a temperature of 87°, the true reading is 29 seconds, as higher temperature has speeded up rennet action by 4 seconds. Fresh milk and heat-treated milk will give a reading of approximately 30 seconds. Milk during ripening, maintained at 85°, will gradually give a quicker test, and after 1-1½ hours may have reduced to approximately 25 seconds. This is sufficient for semi-hard cheese.

Both the acidimeter and rennet test are optional. The small scale cheese-maker can generally rely on time, taste and smell.

Addition of colour (optional)

Annatto is added in the proportions of 1 dm: 8 gallons of milk for light colouring, and 1 dm: 4 gallons for the 'red' of Cheshire type. It must be added 10 minutes before renneting, to ensure complete mixing.

Measure the amount required in a graduated measuring glass. Add direct to milk by plunging it *under* the surface, and then mix in very thoroughly.

Addition of rennet

Standard rennet extract is added in the proportions of 1 dm: 2½-4 gallons milk, according to variety of cheese, but 1 dm: 2-2½ gallons may be required if the milk has been heat-treated, to prevent a soft curd.

Measure the amount required in a graduated measuring glass, immediately before using. Dilute it with 2-3 times its volume of cold water. This does not affect the strength of the extract, but it is for the purpose of easier mixing.

Check the temperature of the milk, which should be between 85°-95°F., according to the variety of cheese.

Add the diluted rennet by pouring quickly on to the milk, and stir it in immediately throughout the depth of the milk for four

When the milk is at the correct temperature for the type of cheese being made, the rennet can be added, and stirred in thoroughly, but not roughly.

42

minutes, to ensure even mixing of the extract. Avoid rough stirring, as this churns out fat. Then 'top stir' the surface of the milk to a depth of approximately ¼ inch either by hand, or by means of some type of stirrer. Continue top stirring until coagulation occurs, otherwise the fat globules rise to the surface, and instead of being trapped in the curd, are subsequently lost in the whey.

Coagulation takes from 10-30 minutes, according to the variety of cheese, but averages 12-20 minutes for semi-hard types. When the milk begins to feel denser to the touch, and bubbles stay on the surface, instead of breaking, curdling is about to occur. Check by carefully letting a drop of cold water fall on to the surface. If the drop spreads, continue top stirring. If stirring is continued after coagulation, the surface of the curd is spoilt by flakiness.

Cover the container with a lid, or clean cloth, and leave until the curd is sufficiently firm. This may be from 30-60 minutes, and is termed the period of coagulation.

Examine the curd at intervals, and do not leave too long, or the whey begins to separate out as a greenish fluid round the edges, and in pools on the surface as the curd contracts. Test the curd by placing the hand flat on the surface and press gently. Insert a finger to a depth of one inch, push it forward, and out, to split the curd. The curd is still too soft if it sticks to the hand, or forms a soft flaky split.

It is ready for cutting if the hand comes away clean, if the curd gives an even split, and if it pulls away from the sides of the container. It must be remembered that the period of coagulation is abnormally rapid if the milk is too hot, or too acid. It is proportionately slower if the milk loses temperature, has been heat-treated, or is not sufficiently acid.

Cutting and scalding of curd

The curd is cut when sufficiently firm, and for semi-hard cheese may be cut by orthodox curd knives, or by the household carver type of knife. The semi-hard cheeses require considerable curd drainage, and it is necessary to break up the curd into suitably sized particles so that whey can escape from them. There is rapid separation after cutting into typical curds and whey, and this separation is further aided by the scalding, or 'cooking' process. The curd is gradually dried, the particles shrinking in size as the whey is lost from them. This shrinkage by drainage must not be too rapid, or the curd becomes tough and dry. The time taken varies according to the eventual moisture and the type of texture required in the cheese. The cut curd must therefore be heated carefully and slowly, and be stirred gently and constantly throughout the heating process. This is to ensure all particles being evenly heated, and to prevent them sticking together. Rough treatment will break up the curd, and cause loss of fat into the whey. The semi-hard varieties do not require much rise in temperature or in acidity and at the end of the scalding period the curd should not be too firm or tough, but slightly flaky.

Methods of cutting

1. (a) *Using American curd knives* (one with vertical blades and one with horizontal blades) where milk has been coagulated in a square or rectangular vessel.

Commence with the vertical knife and cut across the curd lengthways. Slope the knife in and slide it out at each stroke, and continue till all the curd has been cut, overlapping the previous cut as little as possible. Cut with the same knife but crossways, so that the curd shows criss-cross lines on surface. The vertical blades have now cut it into long vertical strips.

Then take the knife with horizontal blades and cut lengthways only. Do not remove knife at each stroke, but slide it along the side of the container and cut through all the curd. The horizontal cutting of the vertical strips forms cubes of curd.

(b) *Using American curd knives* when milk has been coagulated in a circular vessel.

Commence with the vertical-bladed knife and cut across the curd both ways. If any parts of the curd remain uncut, owing to shape of

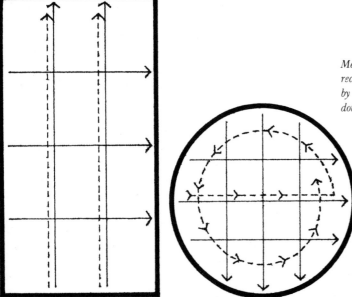

Method of cutting the curd with American curd knives in a rectangular or round vessel. First cut with vertical blades as shown by the solid arrow, then with horizontal blades as shown by the dotted arrows.

container, they can be cut with an ordinary carving knife held vertically. Then take the horizontally-bladed knife and cut through the curd across the middle of the container. Do not withdraw the knife, but with a quick movement draw the knife through the curd spirally, keeping bottom of knife on base of container. The curd is cut into cubes, and any uncut curds can later be cut through with an ordinary knife when the curd is stirred.

2. *Using an ordinary carving knife*

This is done in the same way, whatever the shape of the container. Hold the knife with the blade vertically and cut across both ways, leaving ½-1 inch spacing between the cuts. Then hold the blade horizontally and slide it under the surface of the curd. Cut through and gently raise the cut part of the curd with one hand, or by means of a flat skimmer. As it is raised, cut another horizontal slice below it with the blade, and continue until all the curd is cut through. The particles are not so even in size by this method, but a rough cubing of the curd is obtained.

After cutting, leave the curd for the time advised, to allow some separation of whey, then turn it over very carefully to avoid breaking up the particles.

Scalding or cooking Heating to the required temperature in small containers can be done by two methods—equally satisfactory if care is taken. The temperature and time required depend on the variety of cheese.

Method 1. Fill a quart measure or similar sized vessel with hot water. Suspend this from the side of the tub in the curd, while continuing to stir. Heat is transferred from hot water to the curds and whey. Control the amount and time of heating by a floating thermometer.

Method 2. When sufficient whey has separated, scoop about a quart into a vessel, and heat it by holding the vessel in hot water till the whey has reached 100°-110°F. Pour this heated whey back into the curd, and continue to stir. Repeat the process as required for the time and temperature given in the appropriate recipe. Do not add very hot whey, as it toughens the curd particles with which it comes in contact.

Never try to hurry the heating process. It is always better to heat slowly at first, and to increase the rate towards the end of the scald. The exception to this treatment is when cooking curds of Dutch types of semi-hard varieties. In this case, remove a measured amount of whey at intervals according to time given, and replace with the same quantity of water at the same temperature. This gradually dilutes the whey, which 'washes' the curd. This specialised treatment reduces acidity, and results in the characteristic mild flavour and smooth texture of this type of cheese.

Pitching and drawing the whey

Pitching denotes the settling of curd in the whey. The presumed derivation of the word is interesting, as it originally meant the pitching, or throwing down of the curd. Circular containers were used, and the curd was swirled round in the whey until it rose as a cone in the centre. It could then be trapped in a cloth, and pitched, or allowed to settle, massed towards the centre of the tub. The same method is still used in some continental cheese manufactures, though only the term survives in English practice. The pitching period for the semi-hard cheese need only be sufficient to consolidate the loose curd, as little acid development is required. The whey can therefore be taken off as required, care being taken to avoid wastage of curd.

To remove the whey, tie a cloth over a bucket or container, and tip the curds and whey through the cloth. Do this gently, as rough tipping breaks the curd.

If the curd container is difficult to handle or tip, dip out curds and whey from it, and pour carefully through a stretched cloth over a second container. Tie up the corners of the cloth, one round three, and so form a bundle of curd. Replace in the empty container. If extra drainage is required, place the bundle on a rack, or inverted plate, to prevent the curd standing in accumulated whey. Leave the curd to 'mat' in the bundle before further handling.

Handling the curd in the container

The period following removal of the whey is required for drainage of the curd, with varying

The curds are wrapped in a cloth and left to drain. Curd is usually removed from the cloth for salting and breaking, the pieces being about the size of a small walnut. The frequency of breaking varies with the type of cheese being made and the dryness and texture desired.

degrees of acidity in development. The acidity is controlled by the amount of whey retained in the curd, so the method of handling the curd depends on the degree of drainage required. It also affects the type of texture desired.

Methods Open up the bundle of curd, and proceed as directed in the recipe. If making a close-textured cheese, cut with a sharp knife across the matted curd, to form four inch blocks. Turn the blocks, and re-tie in cloth. To obtain a 'short' texture, cut the blocks and then break them across by hand. Do not re-cut, but break the blocks each time further drainage is required. When a dry cheese is wanted, cut, or break, the curd more often. If it begins to smell too acid, or if it looks stringy, and feels slimy and soft, drain it more vigorously to check the acid. Cut or break into smaller pieces, turn them over frequently, and leave top off container to cool the curd.

Conversely, if a moist cheese is required, or when the curd remains too sweet, handle it less frequently, and keep the blocks larger in size.

Milling or breaking the curd This is necessary to break up the pieces of matted curd so that they can be pressed together in the moulds to the required shape and size of cheese. Special mills are used for large scale work, but for small curds, hand breaking is satisfactory.

Method Weigh the curd, then break it cleanly, without squeezing out fat, into small pieces. If the curd seems very hot, and feels wet and sticky, turn the pieces over several times to drain and cool. This prevents the fat from squeezing out when the curd is subsequently pressed. If the weather is cold, and the curd has lost temperature, complete the breaking process as quickly as possible, as cold curd will not consolidate easily.

Salting and moulding the curd

Most of the semi-hard cheeses are salted after breaking and before moulding the curd. Some types are not salted in the curd, the pressed cheese being placed in brine the following day.

Method If curd is to be salted, weigh out dry salt in proportion of 1 oz. to 3-4 lb. curd. Sprinkle it on broken curd, and mix it in thoroughly. If salt is rough, rub it through a sieve on to the curd as lumps of salt can form blemishes in the cheese.

The term moulding denotes the filling of curd into the cheese moulds or hoops, according to the variety being made. Moulds have fused bases, hoops are open both ends. (There is a confusion of terminology, as in some areas the process is known as vatting, when the moulds are known as vats. In other places, a vat does not denote a cheese mould, but is the actual milk container in which the cheese is made. In the northern parts of Britain, a cheese mould can also be used to describe the addition of prepared mould cultures to a curd, to promote mould growth in a blue veined type of cheese.)

Method Unless otherwise stated, line the moulds with fine cloth, allowing sufficient overlap to fold over the top. Put smaller pieces of curd at bottom and top to obtain an even coat, or rind. Pack in the intervening curd as firmly as possible to top of mould. If making several cheeses, check-weigh the filled moulds, to equalise the weight and size of the cheeses.

Fold lining cloth over top of curd, place the metal or wood follower on top of the cloth, and remove to a level table or shelf where the filled moulds can be pressed. Remember that

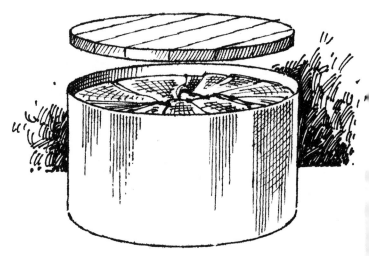

drainage of whey increases under pressure, so that suitable containers must be placed to receive it.

Pressing the cheese

Sufficient pressure to consolidate the curd is neccessary, forming the texture required. The time under pressure, and the weight given, varies with size and type of cheese. The period for semi-hard cheeses is from 12-24 hours.

When no cheese press is available, satisfactory results can be given by dead-weight pressure, using ordinary metal weights of from 4-14 lb. These are placed on top of the mould follower. Press for advised time, then knock out the cheese, turn, and replace in cloth and mould. If curd is not matting well, turn more often to equalise pressure and drainage, and apply extra weight. Be sure an even smooth coat has formed on the cheese before leaving it for final pressure period.

Finishing

This term denotes the final preparation of the cheese for store or disposal. A well finished cheese looks more attractive, and keeps better. An essential part is to prevent excessive surface evaporation, as this can cause the coat of a cheese to crack, and it may also lose an abnormal amount of weight, and become hard and dry. Coating the surface with hot wax, as commonly seen on Dutch cheese, is too difficult a process for the small cheese-maker. He must therefore rely on greasing, bandaging, or both.

Methods 1. Remove pressed cheese from mould, and trim off any rough or uneven edges with a

There are several small presses on the market, but household weights can be used instead, resting on the mould follower. The whey drips into a pan beneath the mould.

49

After the top and bottom of the cheese are 'capped' with cloth, the side bandage is put on, flour and water paste applied and the seam oversewn.

sharp knife. Cut a piece of 'cheese grey' or fine cloth to fit round the cheese, allowing an overlap of one inch at seam, and over top and bottom of cheese. Make an ordinary flour paste, mixed with cold water, and thickened by adding boiling water. Paste surfaces of cheese, and pull bandage tightly round. Stick down side, top, and bottom overlaps. Over-sew the bandage seam with strong thread, pulling stitches tightly.

2. Melt some good quality fat, such as lard, butter, or margarine, by holding it in a container in hot water. Be absolutely sure that the fat cannot affect the cheese in flavour or colour. Rub the melted fat over all surfaces of cheese in a very thin layer, as if too thick it may spoil appearance, or give a rancid taste to the rind after storage.

If the cheese is to be stored for several (4-8) weeks, bandage the greased cheese, as the bandage will give extra protection. It can be stripped off cleanly before final decoration or sale. If the cheese is to be consumed fairly soon, grease it only, but rub it over at intervals with a cloth, as surface mould growth may occur.

Ripening and storage

The semi-hard cheese can be stored to ripen for a period from 2-8 weeks, according to size and variety. The place chosen should be fairly cool, a satisfactory temperature range being 55°-60°F. If too hot, the fat sweats in the cheese. It must not be too dry, or the cheese may lose too much moisture. It must not be too humid, as mould growth may occur on damp surfaces of the cheese. This group of cheeses will undergo some degree of ripening from the action of micro-organisms, causing a gradual softening of texture. The production of a cheesy flavour

succeeds the acid taste, but it must be realised that the small semi-hard cheese cannot acquire the strong flavour of the large hard-pressed Cheddar, Cheshire, etc. The flavour remains fairly mild, but can be extremely palatable.

The storage life is limited by the small size of the cheese; there is a relatively greater surface evaporation than in a large cheese, so that the cheese dries out more quickly, which incidentally checks the ripening action. When ready for consumption, the cheese texture should be sufficiently firm to cut, but not tough. It should be mellow, but not greasy, either inside or outside.

Handling during storage Place your cheeses on a dry, clean wooden shelf or table, where air can circulate freely, but avoid direct draughts. Turn them over daily, to ensure even evaporation, and to prevent them from sticking to shelves. Wipe over with a cloth if necessary, to remove moulds growing on rinds. Clean all the shelves or tables thoroughly before re-use for a further lot of cheese. Scrub the wood with soda, soap, or detergent, and finally wipe over with hypochlorite solution if available.

The semi-hard group is the best one for the small maker who can afford time for manufacture, and a certain outlay in utensils. Cost can however be reduced by intelligent modifications. It is the only group with storage properties over one week's duration, and during storage, little attention or work is involved. The finished small cheese is very attractive for table or sale. It can be consumed raw, or cooked, though for the latter the flavour is inclined to be mild. It also lends itself to the addition of special flavourings by herbs, etc.

Greek Fetta cheese made from goat's milk.

Goat's milk can be used for semi-hard cheese, especially for the Farm-pressed type. The milk must be absolutely fresh. Some goaty flavour may be more apparent in this type of cheese than with soft cheeses, as it develops on storage owing to the chemical nature of the acids.

RECIPES

Miniature Cheshire type
This is made from full-cream milk and 1 gallon yields approximately 18-20 oz. curd. The cheese can be one or two pounds in weight. The use of an acidimeter is optional, but the required acidity figures at different stages are given here (in brackets) in case they are desired.

51

Heat-treatment of milk is optional, but if practised, starter is required. If raw milk is used, evening and morning milk must be mixed to give some initial acidity.

Method Heat up the raw milk to 85°F.: (if previously heat-treated, cool down to 85°F., and add one pint starter to ten gallons milk). Leave milk to ripen for 45 minutes (0.18%). Mix in annatto (optional) in proportion 1 dm : 4 gallons milk. Mix in the rennet in proportion 1 dm : 2½ gallons raw milk, *or* 1 dm : 2 gallons milk if previously heat-treated. Top stir till coagulation has occurred. Leave curd in covered container for 40-60 minutes, according to rate at which the curd firms. Cut the curd when it gives correct reactions for firmness. If using curd-knives, cut lengthways and cross-ways with vertical blades, and lengthways only with horizontal. If using ordinary knife, cut and slice horizontally till curd particles are in ¼-½ inch cubes (0.11-0.12%), taking care not to break up the curd.

Begin stirring very carefully by hand, and be sure that all curd is gently moved, and that the whey can separate out evenly. Continue stirring, and at the same time raise the temperature very gradually, taking 60 minutes to reach the temperature of 93°F. To ensure that the heating is not too rapid, take the temperature of the whey at cutting, calculate the number of degrees to raise it to 93°F., and divide this number by three. Raise a third of the total in the first thirty minutes of the scalding period, and two-thirds in the second thirty minutes. For example, if the temperature of the whey is 84°F. at cutting stage, requiring a total of 9° to reach 93°F., raise the temperature three degrees (to 87°F.) by the end of the first thirty minutes, and a further 6° (to 93°F.) by the end of the second thirty minutes. Continue stirring at 93°F. until the curd particles separate out easily if a handful is shaken in the palm.

Let the curd pitch and settle in the container for fifteen minutes (0.135%). Dip out, or pour off, the whey. Cut a channel down the centre of the curd, and pile it up each side of a rectangular container or at one side of a circular one. Leave the curd for five minutes to allow it to mat together. Cut into five-inch blocks, and carefully turn over each block. Repeat twice, at ten minute intervals. Then break each block by hand, being careful not to crush the curd, but to fracture it across to show the grain of the texture. Turn and break blocks at twenty minute intervals, three times in all (0.22%). Curd should be fairly firm and drained, but not tough. The breaking helps to form the characteristic friable texture. If the curd seems to be getting too dry and tough, break less frequently, and if it seems wet and soggy, break down and turn more often.

When the curd is sufficiently drained, and has a faintly acid taste and smell, break the blocks into small pieces, about the size of filbert nuts. Avoid crushing the curd, or fat will squeeze out. When all curd is broken, sprinkle salt over it, in proportion of 1 oz. to 3½ lb. curd. Mix in the salt thoroughly, and stir up the curd to cool and aerate it. Pack the 'milled' curd by hand into the moulds, which have been lined with fine cloth. Place small pieces at bottom and top, to give a smooth coat. Press down thoroughly, and weigh the filled moulds so that all hold the same amount of curd.

Fold the cloth overlaps over the top of the curd, and place the followers on top. Remove the filled moulds to a level place for drainage. Place weights on top of followers on each mould, approximately 2 lb. on one-pound cheeses, and 4 lb. on two-pound cheeses. If a number of cheeses are to be pressed, place a board over the lot, and weight with 28 lb. or 56 lb. according to size, for twelve cheeses. After one hour, remove the cheeses from the moulds, turn them, and replace in cloth-lined moulds under pressure for a further 12-18 hours, by which time a smooth rind should be formed, and the shape of the cheese be satisfactory. If the cheese appears rough after first turning, turn again an hour later, and, if necessary, increase the weights.

When pressing is finished, paste on bandages, and sew down. Remove to storage room. One pound cheeses are ready for eating or sale after approximately two weeks, and two pounders at four weeks of age.

Caerphilly type

Made from full-cream milk the orthodox Caerphilly size is a flat cheese, height 2½ inches × 10 inches diameter, made from seven gallons of milk. Smaller sizes can be made, either in small cylindrical moulds, or in flat ones such as cake tins. Caerphilly should be eaten within fourteen days of making to obtain the characteristic fresh acid flavour. If stored too long, it becomes dry and harsh. If raw milk is used, mixed evening and morning is best, to give some initial acidity. If milk is heat-treated, starter is necessary. Fresh separated milk can be added in the proportion of ¼, or ⅓, of the volume of milk, but this is only advisable if the cheese is for quick consumption, as separated milk curd soon becomes hard and dry.

Method Heat up the milk to 90°F. (If previously heat-treated, cool down to 90°F., and add one pint starter per 7 gallons milk.) Leave milk to ripen for 45 minutes. Mix in the rennet in proportion of 1 dm : 3½ gallons raw milk *or* 1 dm : 3 gallons if previously heat-treated. Top-stir till coagulation has occurred. Leave curd in covered container for 45 minutes. Cut curd when correctly firm. If using curd-knives, cut lengthways and crossways with vertical blades, and lengthways only with horizontal, to half inch cubes. If using an ordinary knife, cut and slice until particles are approximately half an inch in size.

Turn curd over very carefully, then heat it up as quickly as possible to 92°F., and stir at this temperature for 45 minutes. Press a piece of the curd very carefully, but firmly, with thumb and finger, and when sufficiently firm, an imprint of the skin can be seen on the curd. This is usually apparent after 45 minutes, but if curd is still too soft, continue stirring at 92°F., until imprint is shown. Pitch the curd, and dip or pour off whey immediately. Pile the curd at one side of the container into an even-shaped heap, and leave it for 5 minutes to mat. Slice round the edges of the heap, to a depth of approximately one inch, and pile up the sliced pieces on top of the heap of curd. Cut through as much of the heap as possible, and form a cone of sliced curd. This drains it, and helps to form the characteristic flaky texture. When cone is complete, cut through it with a long knife at one inch spacings, first radially, to form wedges of curd— then horizontally to cut the wedges into long pieces. Spread these pieces of curd along one side, or at one end of container, leaving a channel for the whey to escape. Turn pieces of curd over twice during 10 minutes, by which time it should be fairly dry, but still flaky and soft in texture. Break up by hand, or cut with knife into small pieces about size of filberts. If the cheese is subsequently to be brined, sprinkle on 1 oz. of salt per 7 gallons milk. If it is not to be brined add salt in proportion of 1 oz. to 4 lb of curd.

Pack the curd into the moulds, previously lined with smooth cloth. Pull up collar during filling if using orthodox Caerphilly moulds. Place small pieces of curd at bottom and top of moulds to form smooth coat. Fold over cloth, and press as for Miniature Cheshire if moulded in small sizes. If in an orthodox Caerphilly mould, or cake-tin to make a cheese of three or four pounds weight, use 14 pounds dead weight per cheese. Turn cheese 10 minutes after moulding, and repeat turning at 10 minute intervals once or twice more, until coat is formed. Leave in press for 12-18 hours. Remove from moulds, and place in 20% strength brine for 12 hours if this method of salting is practised. After removal from brine, dry off cheese surfaces, and place in store. Turn daily for 7-14 days. Wipe over coat of cheese, and if for sale, dust over surfaces with dry flour. Rice flour is traditionally used, but can be substituted by wheat flour.

Washed Curd type

There are numbers of European and other cheeses which have a characteristic mild flavour and smooth plastic texture. Many of them have become extremely popular in recent years. Some can be made from small quantities of milk by modified semi-hard cheese methods of manufacture. Buckets, or large containers if required, can be used. The orthodox moulds are sometimes made of wood, to produce round, or flat cheeses, as seen in the Dutch types. Metal moulds can be used quite satisfactorily, though they do not retain the curd temperature so well. For small scale work, any flat metal mould, such as for Caerphilly, or a cake-tin, can be used. Owing to the plastic nature of the curd texture, this type of cheese bulges to form rounded sides. It is therefore inadvisable to use cylindrical moulds, unless they are filled to half capacity only. If made too high, the bulging may cause the cheese to split. Small flat cheeses of from one to four pounds in weight are quite satisfactory. Full-cream sweet milk is used, the yield of cheese being approximately one pound to the gallon.

Method (using three gallons or more) First heat-treat the milk to 150°F., as raw milk may give trouble with gas holes in the curd. Cool to 90°F., and add half a pint of starter to 5 gallons of milk. (If impossible to heat-treat, use raw milk, heat to 90°F., inoculate with starter, and ripen for 30 minutes.) Mix in annatto (optional) in proportion 1 dm : 6 gallons milk. Mix in the rennet in the proportion of 1 dm : 3 gallons milk. Top stir till coagulated. Leave in covered container for one hour. Cut or slice the curd into approximately quarter inch particles, as in Miniature Cheshire method. Heat up curd to

100°F., taking 30 minutes to raise temperature, and retain it at 100° for a further 30 minutes, continuing to stir throughout the 60 minutes. *Additionally,* at 15 minute intervals during the hour, scoop out the whey in the proportion of approximately one quarter of the amount of milk being used, and replace with water at 100°F. For example, if using 6 gallons of milk in a tub or metal container, remove 1½ gallons whey, and replace with 1½ gallons water, every 15 minutes. If using 2½ gallons milk in a bucket, scoop out approximately 5 pints whey and replace with water every 15 minutes.

This gradual replacement of whey with water washes the curd, thus reducing acidity. The process physically alters the curd, causing it to become plastic, so that the resulting cheese is of sweeet mild flavour and soft smooth texture.

After the 60 minutes of scalding and washing, the curd should feel rubbery and elastic when pressed in the hands. At this stage, remove the watery whey, and during removal press down the loose curd by means of a rack, tray, or plate, on which is placed a weight. The absence of acidity in the curd makes it difficult for it to mat unless pressed together. After removing whey, leave the curd under pressure for a further 10 minutes. Then cut out pieces of the matted rubbery curd, as near as possible to size of moulds being used. Place entire piece into mould, lined with fine cloth, and press down thoroughly. Press with a 2 lb. weight on one-pound cheese, and 4 lb. on two-pound cheese, and proportionately more on larger ones. Turn twice in lined moulds at 20 minute intervals, to form smooth coat. Leave under pressure 3-4 hours for smaller cheese, and 6-8 hours for larger. Remove from moulds, and float cheese

in 20% brine for 3–4 hours, 6–8 hours for larger. Remove from brine tank, and place on fine cloth to dry off. Choose a smooth place on which to keep the cheese, as the plastic texture will take imprints, or become distorted very easily. Remove from cloth as soon as dry, place on wooden board or shelf, and turn and rub surfaces daily for 7-10 days. As soon as the coat has dried off evenly to a darker shade, with no damp patches evident, rub surfaces very thoroughly to remove any mould growth. Then rub in a thin coating of melted fat, or olive oil, in place of the hot wax dip, which is the commercial method. Rub surfaces of cheese when turning, every day throughout storage. The small cheeses are ready for consumption in 2-3 weeks, the larger in 4-8 weeks.

When using only 1-2 gallons, the process is the same as when dealing with larger quantities, except that the washing process can be simplified to suit the small amount being handled. After the curd is cut, stir and heat it to 100°F., taking 30 minutes. Then pour off as much whey as possible, and replace it with the same amount of water at 100°F. Continue to stir for a further 30 minutes.

Pressed 'Farm' Cheese ('Smallholder' type)
This is easy to make when only home apparatus is available, and a good method of using from 2-6 gallons of milk. The cheese is suitable for home consumption, and will store for 3-6 weeks according to size. If kept longer, more flavour is developed, but the cheese tends to become dry.

55

Method Use mixed evening and morning milk, so allowing some initial acidity to develop overnight. Heat milk to 90°F. Mix in rennet in proportion of 1 dm : 3 gallons of milk. Leave in covered container for 45 minutes, or until curd is ready. Slice curd into particles of ¼-½ inch size. Turn over carefully, then stir for 30 minutes, meanwhile raising the temperature to 100°F. Settle the curd, and dip or pour off the whey. Scoop the curd into a coarse linen cloth. Gather together three corners of the cloth, and twist the fourth round them, thus forming a bundle. Leave the curd in bundle for 60 minutes, but every 15 minutes tighten the cloth by pulling the fourth corner more tightly round the other three. This expels whey gradually and evenly. At the end of this hour, curd should be firm but flaky. Break up the curd into small pieces, approximate size of filberts, sprinkle and mix in dry salt in proportion of 1 oz. salt : 3 gallons milk. Press the salted curd into mould or cake-tin lined with fine cloth, insert follower, and place a 14-28 pound weight on top, according to size of cheese. Turn cheese into lined mould after 3 hours of pressure, and if rough and insufficiently pressed, increase weight.

On the following day, turn cheese again, and replace under increased pressure—up to 56 lb. for large sized cheese, for 12-24 hours. Remove cheese from moulds, paste on bandage, and sew down. Remove to store and turn daily.

The semi-hard cheeses of farm pressed type will sometimes blue satisfactorily, provided they do not dry out too much before the internal mould growth can develop. To facilitate blueing in such cheese, the curd must be fairly moist, the texture more open than usual, and the cheese ripened in a humid atmosphere (90-95% humidity). A cool cellar, with a temperature of 50°-55°F. is suitable. Humidity can be maintained by swilling the floor with water. Small blue cheeses can also be made from goat's milk, as the extra fat helps to give the characteristic flavour.

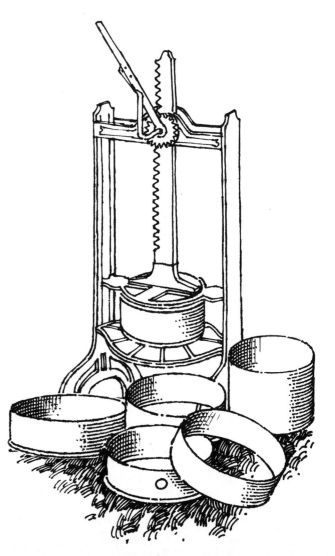

4 MAKING SOFT AND ACID~CURD CHEESE

Soft Cheese

The manufacture of British varieties of soft cheese is much simpler than for the semi-hard types, and well suited to home cheese-making. Some outlay on small equipment is necessary, but much of it can be adapted from available household utensils.

The number of hours required for making soft cheese is relatively small, so that work can be fitted in conveniently with other things. The premises required must have as even a temperature as possible, preferably 65°-70°F. Cold damp rooms are not suitable, nor are hot dry ones, because of the effect on curd drainage. Sufficient space must be allowed for the cheese during the in-hoop and out-of-hoop stages, which require 3-5 days for the unripened varieties. Level shelving, benches and tables must be available, on which to place the cheeses during this period, and where they can be handled and turned without difficulty or damage. The soft curds are easily spilt during early stages, and hoops will slide or tip on a sloping or uneven surface. Considerable whey escapes, so vessels are required to catch the drainings.

Much confusion exists on the subject of soft cheese, and to avoid disappointment it should

be emphasised that the home cheese-maker should not attempt to make the ripened varieties. These are typified by innumerable French and other European varieties, such as Camembert. Such cheese requires specialised facilities for culture growth, and for ripening, which is beyond the scope of the small maker. Ripened soft cheeses undergo completely different chemical changes from those occurring in semi-hard cheese. If European varieties such as Coulommier are made in the home, no attempt should be made to ripen them. They should be consumed fresh.

The surviving varieties of British soft cheeses are not ripened, but consumed, or sold, as soon as sufficiently drained. Unripened soft cheeses are characterised by a pleasantly sharp but not over-acid flavour, and have a soft flaky 'spreadable' texture. Soft cheeses have a high moisture content, and consequently deteriorate quickly. It is therefore absolutely essential to use milk of very good hygienic quality, otherwise defects may occur in the cheese. This is especially the case with unripened British varieties, which can easily be spoilt if contamination by micro-organisms causes undesirable fermentations in the curd, or if mould growth develops on the surface during the few days of storage. It is therefore advised that the milk should be heat-treated, in the manner described on page 33 . This is quite a simple matter, as for soft cheese small quantities of milk are used. A bucket containing 2 gallons of milk, sufficient for 4 cheeses of approximately 1 pound each in weight, is perfectly easy to handle. The composition of the milk is not so important for curd-formation as with semi-hard types, as a softer coagulum is suitable. Soft-cheese milk can safely contain a higher fat content, up to 4.5%, because there is less danger of its loss during cheese-making. Milk with a fat content below 3.5% is liable to give hard, dry cheese. Cleaning and sterilisation of all equipment is absolutely necessary, and any carelessness on this point may lead to disaster. The equipment is all of small size, so boiling it in water presents no difficulty. Special care must be taken with wooden boards, straw mats, and cloths, all of which can harbour contaminants. Moulds and yeasts can be especially troublesome, and it is useless to cut out contaminants in the milk, only to contaminate the curd or cheese subsequently during the draining stages.

Sequence of processes
Treatment of the milk
Addition of rennet
Slicing and dipping of curd
Drainage in-hoop
Salting
Drainage out-of-hoop

Treatment of milk

Developed acidity is not required for soft cheese manufacture, though a proportion of

lactic acid-producing micro-organisms is a desirable safeguard against contaminants. Cooled evening's milk is suitable, if it is held overnight at a low temperature, and can be made into cheese the following morning. The interval will give time for some lactic organisms to devlop, but care must be taken that the milk does not ripen excessively, as acid milk spoils the cheese. If morning's milk is used the yield of cheese is smaller than with evening's, and the texture may become harsh and dry. Mixed milk is quite satisfactory. The use of starter is not essential, unless the milk is heat-treated, when small inoculations are required. In cases where heat-treatment is thought to be necessary, the use of starter could be advantageous. In this event, keep milk in a cool place in a covered, sterile bucket or container, till used. Heat-treat the milk to 150°F., remove from the hot water immediately temperature is reached, and cool by placing the container of milk in running ccld water. Cool to between 90°-95°F., according to directions. Add starter at this temperature at the rate of half a drachm to each gallon of milk.

Alternatively, if the milk is considered safe, omit the heat treatment, and raise the temperature of milk direct to 90°-95°F. Keep milk, and curd throughout manufacture, in a warm place, approximately 65°-70°F.

Addition of rennet

No ripening of the milk is required, so rennet can be added immediately the correct temperature is reached. Standard cheese rennet is used, the coagulation process being similar to that in semi-hard cheese. The difference is the production of a softer curd, by using a smaller proportion of rennet on a 'sweeter' milk. The process is consequently slower, and the time for coagulation and forming of curd is proportionately longer.

Measure out the rennet in drachm glass according to the recipe being used. Dilute to six times its volume with cold water. Mix into milk very thoroughly. Top-stir until coagulation has occurred. Cover bucket or container, and leave undisturbed for time prescribed, or until curd is sufficiently firm to handle. Sterilise boards, hoops and mats, and leave in hot water until curd is ready.

Slicing of curd and in-hoop drainage

The soft cheeses do not require drastic drainage, consequently the curd is not usually cut. Fairly large pieces of curd are retained, which must be allowed to pack down slowly in the hoops. This is done by slicing or scooping out the curd direct from the coagulum, by means of a scoop or skimmer. These portions are transferred carefully to the hoops, drainage being accelerated if slicing is thin, and vice versa. The whey is expelled by natural gravity, no pressure being given at any stage. Consequently the rate of drainage is very dependent on temperature, as the curd contracts more at a higher range, and retains whey at a lower. It is essential to maintain the temperature of making (approximately 65°-70°) throughout preliminary drainage. If the milk has lost much heat, or if the curd is chilled during ladling and in-hoop stages, the whey is expelled too slowly; the curd does not sink in the hoop, and filling and turning is delayed.

Method Remove the hoops, mats and boards from the hot water and assemble them. Test the curd for firmness—it is ready if it will leave the sides of the container when pulled away with the finger. Take the metal scoop, skimmer, or spoon out of the hot water. If 'tops' are required for the cheese, cut out size by pressing hoop on to surface of curd, scoop out cut piece with a skimmer, and slide it on to a clean saucer. Leave these saucers in a safe place, where the tops will not be disturbed.

Ladle out remainder of the curd in container by means of a scoop or spoon, taking even, fairly thin slices, and placing them carefully in the prepared hoops. Do not break up the curd more than can be helped, as this causes wastage of fat and curd.

Fill hoops to top, and then leave for a period to allow sinkage of curd. This can be hastened by dipping out whey from the top. Continue filling with curd as space allows until all is used. Slide the curd top from the saucer on to filled hoop by a quick, deft movement. Leave the hoops in a warm place for approximately twelve hours, to allow whey drainage to continue.

Out-of-hoop drainage and salting

This drainage usually commences 12-24 hours after filling, but varies with the type of hoop, and rate of curd drainage. With double hoops, which are constructed of two fitting sections, the top section is removed when the curd has sunk to that level. Total removal of hoop is seldom possible before 48 hours after filling. If drainage is checked by cold room temperature, the filled hoops, on the mats and boards, can be removed for a short period to a warm room, such as the kitchen. This has practical difficulties, and should be regarded as an emergency measure.

Method On the day after making, boil the required number of boards and straw mats. Allow mats to dry. Place a mat across the top of the hoop, then a board on top of the mat. Put one hand under board on which cheese is standing, place the other hand on the board over the top, and reverse the whole, holding all the apparatus firmly. If desirable, sprinkle salt over newly exposed surface of curd, and leave to drain for a further 12-24 hours.

If the cheese is by then sufficiently firm to keep its shape, remove hoop, and turn the cheese on to a freshly prepared straw mat and board. Sprinkle salt over newly exposed surface of cheese. If the straw mat tends to stick, and pull away the the surface of the cheese, stretch the mat from end to end before turning. This separates out the straws, and releases them from intervening curd.

Continue to turn cheese daily for several days until it is sufficiently firm to handle without breaking.

Most varieties require turning daily to equalise drainage, and some are slightly salted during this stage. Clean dry salt is sprinkled lightly over the exposed surfaces for the first two turnings. Too much salt dries out the cheese and spoils the flavour. Some varieties are not salted at any stage. Salting is largely a matter of taste, but it must always be remembered that 'a little goes a long way' and it is much easier to over-salt than under-salt. If soaking in brine is advised, care must be taken to leave for a maximum period of 30 minutes, otherwise too much salt is absorbed, and the flavour and texture spoilt. During the period of 2-5 days, when the cheese is completing drainage, there is a tendency for the wet surfaces to become covered with a growth of mould. This is not required for unripened varieties, and gives an unsightly appearance. It also reduces sales value, as although such moulds are entirely harmless to the consumer many people imagine that mouldy cheese is 'bad'. The following measures are advisable during final stages of draining.

If the cheese shrinks considerably, remove to a cooler room such as a cellar or larder. If mould grows copiously on the surface, wipe cheese over with a cloth dipped in cold water. Dry off, and remove to a colder, drier place. Always consume or sell unripened varieties as soon as they are firm. When the cheese is fairly dry and firm, wrap it in greaseproof paper or transparent material. Remember that wrapping is inadvisable if the cheese is to remain in its covering for several days as moulds will grow under the wraps, and give an unsightly appearance. Wrapping must be considered as a short-time hygienic protection, or as a means of enhancing sales value. For consumption in the home, keep the cheese in an open dish, lightly covered with grease-proof paper. If it tends to dry out, wrap it in damp muslin, but remember that it will then go mouldy quickly.

Marketing and uses

Unripened soft cheese is difficult to handle, owing to the high moisture content, and to the tendency for whey seepage into any wrappings or boxes used. Packaging materials to fit specific cheeses can be obtained, but are costly, so these cannot be considered economical unless a fairly large quantity is sold on a market with a steady demand. Special cardboard, or chip-wood, boxes can be printed or labelled, which has further advertising value. The old method of marketing the cheeses was to place them on fresh cabbage or other green leaves. These kept them cool, gave them some protection, allowed drainage, and lent a pleasant appearance. This treatment was suitable for sale at market stalls, and can still be seen in a few localities. It is unsuitable for most methods of modern distribution, but the home table can be enlivened by serving in this way.

Soft cheeses are very digestible, and of high protein content. They are not suitable for cooking purposes, but should be eaten raw, whether as the natural cheese, or mixed with other substances. They have the great advantage of being equally pleasant when accompanied by savoury or sweet foods. The combination of the characteristic acid tang of unripened soft cheese with sweet flavours, has for long been appreciated in Europe. Soft cheese curd can therefore accompany stewed or raw fruit, sugared cereals, or be spread on bread with jam, honey or syrup. The soft flaky curd is easily macerated and pulped, and when mixed with flavourings, whether savoury or sweet, becomes a delicious spread.

Goat's milk is very satisfactory for making soft cheese, providing it is used absolutely fresh. The curd is rich in fat, and therefore may require a longer period for drainage. Slightly more rennet can be used to form a firmer curd to aid expelling the whey. The absence of yellow colour in the fat is misleading, and if desired, this can remedied by adding some annatto.

All soft cheeses are liable to attack by flies while they are draining. Blow flies lay their eggs on soft surfaces, and the maggots which hatch out do great damage. They eat their way into the cheese, causing an obnoxious putrefactive mass. Protection can be given by muslins, impregnated with some hypochlorite (not fly deterrent sprays). The cloths must not actually touch the cheese, as the flies can lay their eggs through them. When any insect spray is used in the premises all milk products must be protected from such contact. A good plan is to place the cheese on shelves, and to fix cloths over the fronts with drawing pins. These can be removed easily when it is wished to turn the cheese.

Any cheese which is soft-coated, such as new semi-hard ones, are liable to fly attack, and should be similarly protected.

Cambridge or York cheese

One and a half gallons full-cream milk make two cheeses of rectangular shape.

Method (using raw milk). Heat milk to 90°F. (If weather is cold, and temperature of curd liable to drop, heat to 92°-94°F.) Mix in rennet, in proportion of 1 dm : 1½ gallons milk.

If a creamy top is required, which is the traditional feature of the cheese, do not top stir, but allow the cream to rise. If a coloured cream slice is desired, take out two pints of the renneted milk, place in a separate container, and add ½ ml. of annatto. Mix in colour thoroughly, and leave to coagulate. Top stir the remaining milk until coagulation occurs. Leave in covered bucket for 1-1½ hours, at an even temperature, until curd is sufficiently firm to 'split over the finger' cleanly. Take the prepared, cleaned and sterilised utensils, and fit together the two parts of the mould. Place a fitting piece of straw mat in each tray, and press down the top part of the mould in to the tray. Stand assembled moulds on the draining table.

Ladling and filling In making cheese with creamy tops, mark correct size by cutting the top of coagulum with a spare mould top. Scoop two pieces off thinly by means of a skimmer, and retain until required for sliding on top of moulds when the ladling is complete. Ladle out thin slices of curd and place carefully and evenly in the two moulds, until they are filled. Leave the curd to drain until it sinks, so that all remaining in bucket can be ladled into moulds. Finally slide the tops on to each mould and leave to drain.

If making cheese with a cream slice through the centre, slice off two tops from surface of coagulum, and retain. Ladle out approximately three quarters of the uncoloured curd into the moulds. Then ladle evenly into each the coloured curd. Fill and top up with the uncoloured curd. When drainage is complete, the curd sinkage allows the coloured slice to appear centrally in the cheese.

Do not turn the moulds. The characteristic appearace depends on the curd curling over from the corners. Do not add any salt, unless especially desired, as the cheese is traditionally unsalted.

When sufficiently drained, in 2-3 days' time, remove the top and tray of mould, but leave cheese on its straw mat. Serve, or sell, on this.

If the surface of the cheese becomes mouldy during drainage, soak up the whey by placing a cut piece of white blotting paper on cheese. This prevents further contamination from the mould spores in the air. Remove paper before serving or selling cheese.

The flavour of Cambridge or York is characteristically sharp and acid, and being unsalted, the cheese can be eaten with sweet or savoury accompaniments.

Colwick cheese

top of coagulum with Colwick hoop, slice off required two pieces for tops, and retain. Line the circular hoops with fine muslin, allowing sufficient overlap to fold over top of curd. Ladle the curd in fine even slices into the hoops, and when all curd is filled in, and sufficiently sunk, slide on the tops. After one hour of draining, pull the cloths up and towards the centre, thus pulling the curd away from the sides of the hoop. Repeat at intervals during first four hours. This produces the characteristic curling over of the curd edges, a traditional feature of Colwick cheese. Do not turn the cheese during draining. After 24-36 hours of draining, the cheese should be sufficiently dry and firm to handle. Remove hoop and carefully pull away the cloth. Salting is optional, but if desired, sprinkle a small quantity on surface of cheese.

A Colwick soft cheese hoop, lined with muslin, being filled with curd. The mould stands on a straw mat and wooden board, resting in a tray. On the right is the same cheese after one day in the hoop, showing the characteristic folding-in of the curd edges caused by pulling the muslin upwards and inwards. In the foreground is the finished cheese.

Full cream milk is used and 1½ gallons of milk makes two cheeses of circular shape.

Method Proceed as for Cambridge cheese until rennet is added. Top stir till coagulated, and leave in covered container for 1-1½ hours. Mark

Coulommier cheese

Proceed as for Colwick cheese up to ladelling of curd. Take off three tops and transfer to saucers. (Three cheeses can be made from 1½ gallons of milk.) Ladle into unlined two-part moulds. After about 12 hours carefully remove the top half of the mould, the curd having drained and shrunk below half-way. Place a clean mat and board on top of the cheese and, holding firmly, turn it over. Clean and scald the mat and board which come to the top and replace them to protect the cheese in the mould.

Sprinkle the surface which comes up with a little salt. Repeat turning and salting in 6–8 hours, and turn twice more in the next 24 hours. After two days the cheese should be firm enough to leave the mould. Place on a dry mat, and consume fresh.

Acid-curd Cheese

This group contains all varieties in which the milk is initially coagulated by lactic acid instead of rennet. Curd formed by acid is different chemically and physically from a rennet-formed curd. It is not possible to cut it and retain a particle shape (except under specialised manufacturing methods); an acid curd breaks up into a flocculent mass, which becomes increasingly granular as it drains. Entirely different methods of handling are required, but compared with other types of cheese, acid-curd varieties require very simple methods and apparatus. An exception is the commerical 'cottage cheese' at present being marketed by many dairy firms, which is not suited to small scale manufacture. This is in fact an adaptation of acid-curd cheese, and requires special equipment for the accurate testings of temperature and acidity. The acidity is reduced during making by a washing process, and the final product retains separate curd particles. It is a completely different product to the 'cottager's' cheese, which consists of a lactic acid curd, with no separate particles, and a granular but spreadable texture. It is possible that the old name has been adapted to the commercial manufacture.

Cottager's cheese simply denotes any form of acid-curd made from soured milks. It is the type so often recommended to the housewife as a means of avoiding waste, and to the farmer's wife for making use of rejected and returned milk. As previously mentioned, this theoretical recommendation is of no practical value if the milk is old and tainted. Lactic acid types are dependent on a clean acid fermentation, so the maker must decide whether the milk in question is worth using. It is also essential to realise that large quantities cannot be handled unless special facilities exist. The methods require a lot of space for draining of the curds, and it is quite impossible to make large amounts on ordinary house and farm premises. In a few cases there may be sufficient sinks, and curing troughs, to make it feasible, but generally the small maker is limited to a maximum quantity of ten gallons of milk. Any smaller amount can be utilised, as even a pint bottle of sour milk will yield some curd for the home.

The acid-curd cheeses can be made from full-cream milk, skim or separated milks, a mixture of both, milk with added cream, or from surplus starter. The flavour of the acid-curds is characteristically sharp, and the texture is granular but can be spread to a smooth consistency. The smoothness of the texture is largely dependent on the fat content. Full-cream milk curd has a much smoother texture than separated milk curd, as all low-fat acid-curds tend to be rough. Excess heating of soured milk will also increase the roughness. All types should be consumed or sold as soon as sufficiently drained, as in the absence of specialised packing facilities they have a short keeping time. Moulds and yeasts grow on the surface within a few days, and the flavour becomes yeasty and unpleasant instead of cleanly acid.

The use of starter to initiate the lactic fermentation is a means of controlling it, and the curd produced is of the best quality. Starter can only be considered economic if the curds are being made over a definite period. In such a case the carry-over of starter, as previously described, would be worth while.

Practically all the equipment required for manufacture can be modified from that existing in home or farm. The main cost incurred is on the cloths required for draining purposes, whether they are bought for the purpose, or taken from the household linen store.

Sequence of processes
Treatment of the milk
Handling and drainage of the curd
Salting curd
Packing

Treatment of milk

1. *Using soured milk* Check on its quality by taste and smell, and reject it if not clean. If flavour and aroma are pleasantly acid, pour into a sterilised container. Leave container, covered with cloth, in a warm place (60°-65°F.) until a solid coagulum has formed. The time required will obviously depend on the degree of acidity initially present, but sufficient time must always be given for formation of a firm curd, otherwise it is impossible to retain it in the draining cloths.

2. *Using fresh milk* If uncooled, strain into a sterile covered container and leave in a warm place till coagulation is complete.

If cooled, warm the milk up to 70°F. before leaving it to curdle. If souring by starter, warm up to 70° before adding approximately one pint starter per five gallons milk. Stir in thoroughly, then leave in warm place to coagulate. In warm weather, this may occur within 6-12 hours, but if the temperature of the room is low, it will take longer.

Drainage and salting of the curd

Drainage of the whey is by gravity, the rate depending on acidity, temperature, and methods of handling. If the temperature can be maintained consistently, whey expulsion is quicker. If curd can be distributed, or stirred up at intervals, the whey can escape more readily. Drainage can be further hastened by heating up the coagulum to a maximum temperature of 100°F., but this tends to yield a rough-textured product, and is best avoided if possible. Drainage can be effected by two methods. By the first the coagulum is suspended in a tied cloth, and in the second it is spread on cloths stretched over racks. In both cases the curd must be scraped off the cloth, and mixed in, at intervals. This is to prevent the checking of further drainage through the formation of a crust of curd on surfaces against the cloth, as the harder outer curd can entrap the moisture. Salting can be done during the drainage process, preferably when curd is fairly dry, otherwise salt is lost in the whey. Drainage takes 1-3 days, according to conditions, and throughout the process the curd must be kept free from contaminants as far as possible. Cloths must be changed daily, and washed and boiled between use.

Packing

Expensive packing is not necessary unless considerable quantities are being sold. In this case the curd can be pressed down into cartons, boxes or foil cups. Cost is increased, but the keeping period is lengthened, and sales value is greater. For ordinary purposes, the curd can be shaped, or rolled, in muslin, and pressed by hand, between two boards. After shaping it can be wrapped in parchment paper, or transparent coverings. These packs give quite good protection from contamination, but do not protect from the hazards of handling, which can cause loss of shape.

As with the soft cheese, the acid-curd types can be eaten with savoury or sweet substances. They can be flavoured in a variety of ways, and made up into sandwich-spreads. They are not suited to cooking. The cream cheeses are dealt with separately, in Chapter 5, as they are not in fact curd-cheeses, but drained cream. Some of the hybrid types, such as those made from acid curd fortified by extra cream, are inevitably confused with cream cheese proper.

Curd can be hung to drain over any sort of pan or bucket, but if you are making a considerable quantity of acid-curd cheese a rack of this sort is useful and quite easy to make.

Petit Suisse type

When making acid curds from mixed milk and cream, such as for the Petit Suisse type, the process is similar to that for single cream cheese. Use two quarts of fresh, or acid, milk, according to preference. Mix in thoroughly one quart of thin cream (30% fat). Warm up to 65°F., and add ½ ml. of rennet. Stir thoroughly, then leave in covered container in a warm place (60°F.) for 12-15 hours. When coagulum is formed, hang it up in a cloth, but avoid draughts. Treat as for acid curds during drainage. Add one teaspoonful of salt when sufficiently firm. Fill into moulds, or shape by hand. (The orthodox shape for the Petit Suisse type of cheese is cylindrical, the moulds being 2½ inches high × 1¾ inches diameter. They can be obtained with 6, or 12, moulds on one stand, complete with followers.)

Other varieties of soft and acid-curd cheese

If it is wished to make small soft cheese not of the traditional varieties described, the initial coagulum can be produced as for Colwick cheese. This can be ladled out into adapted hoops, made by cutting the bases off tins. Small sized cheeses are then produced, which drain more quickly than the larger, and are therefore ready for consumption in a shorter time.
If *goat's milk* is used, it should be renneted as soon as possible after milking, and ¾ dm rennet added per gallon of milk.

Soft cheese varieties which are not turned during drainage can be finally finished with a layer of clotted cream on the top, spread on immediately before serving, or sale.

Methods of making acid-curd types

Boil all draining cloths, and dry before use. Ensure they are of sufficiently close weave to retain curd, but not so close as to prevent drainage. Examine carefully for holes, as a torn cloth allows undrained curd to flow through. If using the 'bundle' system, spread the cloth over a container, and carefully pour the coagulum into it. Tie up the corners with a slip-knot, and suspend the bag of curd. Be sure that it swings clear of any obstruction. If using rack system, spread cloth over a rack or tray enclosed in some type of frame. Pour in coagulum, and leave to drain.

With both methods, scrape down the coagulum at intervals, using a knife or blade. Scrape from outside inwards, and thoroughly mix the curd. Change the cloths daily to avoid mould and yeast contamination. When drainage is nearly complete, sprinkle in dry salt, in proportion of ¼-½ oz. per pound of curd, and mix in. Package the curd as soon as the consistency is sufficiently firm to handle.

Special flavourings for cheese

All type of home-made cheese can be flavoured if desired, either during manufacture, or when making up the finished cheese into spreads, immediately before serving. When flavouring is added depends on the type of cheese. Semi-hard varieties must be flavoured when curd is broken, and before filling into moulds.

Soft cheese can be flavoured in the initial milk or during the ladling stage into the hoops. Acid-curd types are flavoured during the final mixing at the end of the drainage period. Many flavours can be used, but some are more suitable for cheese than others. Most of them can be grown in the herb garden, and all of them are now available as a dried preparation. The flavour is more pronounced with fresh herbs, and they have the advantage of giving a good colour.

Flavouring and colouring by herbs is an old tradition in the making of some varieties of cheese, especially the 'striped' ones. These have green and white layers, produced by packing in the moulds alternate layers of white and coloured curd, which are subsequently pressed together. The amount of flavouring substances added necessarily depends on their respective strengths, and no hard and fast rules can be laid down. The maker must decide how strongly flavoured he or she wants the cheese, but should remember it is a mistake entirely to mask the initial cheese flavour. It is best to try out a variety of herbs to suit individual tastes.

Some of the flavourings which have proved popular in cheese are sage, celery, garlic, basil, caraway, tarragon, mint, pimento and tomato. Celery and garlic are best added in the salt form, as the amount can be more easily controlled. Caraway seeds are better than caraway flavour, as the seeds are a traditional feature in several varieties of cheese and curd, both in Britain in Europe. If fresh herbs are used, they should be chopped finely, and added with their own juices. When extra green colour is desired, and when colouring curd for striped cheese, the leaves of spinach, kale or sage can be used. Spinach gives the clearest green colour, curly kale is a good second, and sage produces a brownish-green.

To extract the colouring, the fresh leaves are first chopped finely. Boiling water is poured on, and the leaves pressed thoroughly with a wooden spoon. Sufficient water to extract the maximum of plant juices is required, but if too much is added, colour is lost by dilution. The colour is taken up evenly by the curd, and if added at the same time as the salt, and very well mixed in, the pieces of curd are thoroughly coloured before being pressed together in the mould.

All the flavourings mentioned are also suitable for adding direct to spreads, and sandwich fillings. These lend themselves to a greater variety of flavourings, such as mustard, white and red peppers, tomato pulp or ketchup, chutney, cucumber, and Marmite. If spreads are being made from curds of low fat content, spreading quality and flavour are improved by mixing in a proportion of butter or margarine.

68

5 CREAM

This is an important milk product, composed of all the constituents of milk with an excess of milk fat. The proportion of fat present in cream varies with the method of cream production.

Cream can be produced from the milk of all breeds of cows. Milks with the highest fat content are the most economical for cream production. Channel Island cows are particularly suitable for the purpose: the fat percentage of their milk is comparatively high and present in the form of large globules which form a cream easily. The milk fat of these breeds is a good colour at all seasons of the year. Goat's milk contains a high proportion of fat, and good cream can be produced from it. There is no colouring pigment associated with the fat of goat's milk and the cream is white as compared with that from cow's milk. The colour associated with the fat of cow's milk varies, due to factors such as the breed of cow, the food of the cow, the season of the year, and the lactation period. Green food increases the colour of milk fat in any breed. This is noticeable when the cows first go out to grass in the spring. The old saying that the cream and butter are yellow because the cows are eating buttercups is not true, as cows do not eat buttercups. The assumption is understandable because the grass is very lush when the buttercups are in flower.

The variations in the colour of cream is the cause of criticism of the 'cream line' in bottled milk. The housewife appreciates a good cream line, and this is more obvious when the fat in the cream is a good colour. During the winter months milk fat is paler, and the cream line on the milk is less apparent.

Clean milk produced from healthy cows is an essential factor in good cream production. The milk-fat and water are the most variable constituents in cream. An average quality cream, suitable for table use, and for butter-making, has the following approximate composition:*

```
Fat . . . . . . . . . . . . . . . 30-35%
Protein . . . . . . . . . . . . 3-4%
Milk sugar . . . . . . . . . . 3-4%
Ash . . . . . . . . . . . . . 0.4-0.5%
Water . . . . . . . . . . . 64-57%
```

In very thick cream, such as is used in the manufacture of double-cream cheese, the fat percentage may be as high as 50-60% with a corresponding reduction in the other constituents—mainly the water.

Cream production by gravity

This method has been practised for centuries, probably for as long as cow's milk has been used for human consumption. Milk fat is lighter than the other constituents, and a large percentage rises to the surface of the milk if it is left standing for any period of time. This portion of the milk contains a high percentage of fat and can be skimmed off as cream. The thickness, or consistency of cream varies. The causes of the variation can be due to temperature, the length of time allowed for the cream to form on the top of the milk, and the size of the actual fat globules in the milk (due to the breed of cow). The Ayrshire breed produces good quality milk with a fat percentage of 3.5-4.5%. The milk does not form such a thick

* See 1970 No 752 Food and Drugs Composition and Labelling.

70

cream layer as that of the Channel Island breeds, even with a similar fat content. The reason for this is that the fat globules in the Ayrshire milk are small and do not rise to the surface as rapidly as the larger globules. Ayrshire milk is therefore particularly good for cheese-making, as the small fat globules rise slowly and are more effectively held in the curd during rennet coagulation.

The warm milk, straight from the cow, should be poured into a shallow vessel or pan. The construction of these shallow pans is such that the maximum amount of surface is exposed for creaming. They hold 2-3 gallons of milk, the depth of milk not more than 3-4 inches. This pan of milk should be kept for 12-24 hours in a cool, clean atmosphere. The atmosphere in which the cream is exposed should be free from dust; no extraneous matter of any kind should drop into the milk. The pan of milk should never stand near any strong-smelling substance, as flavours will be absorbed.

After 12 hours the cream will have risen to the surface. This can be skimmed off, and should be in the form of a thick layer which can be removed, leaving the milky layer in the pan. The skimming of the cream is done effectively with a perforated skimmer. These thin metal skimmers are easy to handle and to clean. A saucer, or a tablespoon, can however be substituted for this purpose. When only one or two pints of milk are set in a shallow basin for household use, the tablespoon is adequate for skimming. Cream produced in this way is ready for immediate consumption. If sold it can be packaged into cartons, which are hygienic and cheaper than jars.

This simple method of cream production can give excellent results, but the cream must be kept as cold as possible, and should be consumed within a few hours of production unless refrigerated.

Clotted cream

The keeping quality of the cream produced by the gravity method can be increased if the pan of milk is heated after the cream has risen to the surface. Different degrees of heat are applied by different individual producers. Large quantities of this type of heated cream are sold in Britain under the name of scalded cream, clotted cream, Devonshire cream and Cornish cream. The heat kills micro-organisms and if the milk and cream are cooled quickly after heating, the cream and skimmed milk will keep several days longer than the cream produced from raw milk. This is one reason why there is such a large postal trade in scalded and clotted cream.

The traditional farmhouse method was to place the shallow pans of milk, after the cream had risen, on top of the kitchen stove (copper pans were commonly used for heated cream). The stoves, fuelled with peat, ensured that the heating was slow, which is important for the flavour of this type of cream. The cream was considered ready when the surface became wrinkled and a slightly raised circle of cream appeared about an inch from the rim of the container. Modern slow combustion stoves have replaced the peat fires and can be used with success for heating cream. The distinctive flavour of clotted cream is due to the coagulation of some of the proteins of the milk, combined with a slight caramelisation of the sugar of milk. Both these factors are affected by temperature, and time of heating and cooling. When a dairy thermometer is available, heating and cooling can be controlled. Slow heating is essential. The temperature should never be raised to its maximum in less than half an hour, preferably taking one hour or even longer. The cream that has been subjected to high temperature, nearing boiling point, has a thicker and more granular texture, than cream which has been heated to lower temperatures between 150°-170°F. Individual British counties and farms have very definite preferences for particular temperatures, and the thicker clotted cream has always been a product of Devonshire. Many commercial farms produce clotted and scalded cream.

An alternative method of heating 'set' milk is to place the entire pan into a container of water which stands on some stove or other source of heat. Care must be taken not to disturb the cream layer. Heating in a water bath is a satisfactory method, as temperatures can be controlled by means of the water. There is no danger of the pan of milk boiling over, and no risk of the milk burning on the bottom of the pan as may occur in the stove method. Small quantities of milk (1-2 pints) can be heated in a double saucepan, but this is hardly worth the trouble, unless the cream is rich and produces a good cream layer.

Separated cream heated over boiling water for one hour will form a crust on top and approximate to clotted cream, though the flavour is different. After heating by any method the pan of milk and cream must be cooled. The surface must not be disturbed during cooling. Slow cooling to 120°F. in thirty

When making clotted cream the bowl of milk with set cream must be very slowly heated, either directly on the kitchen stove or in a bowl within a pan of hot water.

the year there is less risk of contamination and the cooling is effective if the pan is left on a cold shelf overnight.

After the heating and cooling processes, the cream can be skimmed off the milk. It is in the form of a very thick, almost blankety, layer much more solid in consistency than raw cream. Before skimming, it is advisable to free the cream from the sides of the pan, sliding a knife round the edge of the cream. The layer can be removed by means of a perforated skimmer. If to be filled into small sized containers, the layer of cream on the skimmer can be transferred by a spoon or pastry-cutter. Clotted cream is solid and is always sold by weight. It can be packaged in tins or cartons containing ¼ lb., ½ lb., and 1 lb.

The clotted cream can be removed with a perforated skimmer or a large spoon, and put into a bowl or small cartons for sale.

minutes, then rapid cooling to 45°-50°F. has a good effect on the texture of the clotted cream. It should therefore be cooled by circulating cold water round the pan of milk, or by standing the cream in the coldest available place, such as on a slate or marble slab. The cream could subsequently be cooled in a refrigerator, at a temperature of 36°-40°F. In very hot weather slow cooling is not advisable under farmhouse conditions. Contamination may occur, and the slow cooling may allow micro-organisms to grow which will affect the flavour of the cream. A common defect is the presence of small gas holes in the cream. The flavour of such contaminated cream is bitter and the texture spongy. In the cooler seasons of

Milk with a high fat content is the most profitable for clotted cream manufacture: 2½ gallons of milk containing 3.5% fat will make one pound of clotted cream and 1½-2 gallons of milk containing 4-5% fat will produce one pound of clotted cream.

The packaged cream must be stored in a cool place, and should keep for 24-48 hours after production, and longer if kept in a refrigerator. The skimmed milk also will have a better keeping quality than that produced from raw cream.

Composition of clotted cream

Water	30-40%
Fat	55-60%
Protein	4-5%
Lactose	1-2%
Ash	0.4-0.5%

Making clotted cream Use warm milk as fresh as possible after milking. Pour it into a shallow container with a large surface area. Leave for 12 hours in a cool place, 45°-55°F. Remove the pan of milk with care to a source of heat, disturbing the cream layer as little as possible. Heat slowly, for half an hour to one hour, and raise the temperature to between 160°-200°F; 190°F. is an average temperature. Cool to 50°F. Remove the clotted cream layer and use for home consumption or sale.

Many agricultural shows have competitive classes for all types of cream. If it is decided to enter cream for competition at local shows, strict attention must be given to all details relating to the scheduled conditions of presentation. Cream of any type, presented for judging, should be in clean sound containers. These may be specified on the show schedule; if not, good quality cartons, tins or basins should be used. A plain glass tumbler gives an attractive appearance to liquid cream. Cellophane should cover all open surfaces. Attractive appearance and hygienic wrapping are very important factors. A good quality cream will never gain top marks if packaged badly. A scale of points is used for judging cream; for example:

Flavour	50
Texture	20
Colour	15
Packaging	15

The skimmed milk from gravity cream production, whether raw or heat-treated, contains a percentage of fat, even after twice skimming. This is approximately 0.6-0.7%. The skimmed milk contains the milk proteins and can be used for cooking. It is also good for farm stock and poultry. Skimmed milk can be made into certain types of cheese for home consumption.

Composition of skimmed milk

Water	90%
Protein	3.8%
Fat	0.76%
Lactose	4.68%
Ash	0.76%

Cream production by centrifugal methods

The machine used is known as a centrifugal separator. The constituents of milk vary in their relative density, as is shown in the gravity methods of cream production. The fat is the lightest constituent and has less resistance to force than the heavier milk constituents. The mechanical separator is so constructed that the whole milk is revolved at a high speed in a strong metal container. The light fatty portion, or cream, is held near to the centre of revolution, the heavier portion, or separated milk, being forced furthest from the centre of revolution. The cream and separated milk are forced out of their respective outlets by the pressure of the milk flowing into the machine. The process is continuous.

The use of centrifugal force for the separation of milk components was first attempted mechanically at the end of the nineteenth century. The introduction of this revolutionary method of producing cream received little encouragement from the farming community. The original models were crude in design, and very different in operation from the traditional gravity methods of cream production. The use of mechanical separators is now universal. They have revolutionised cream production, and enabled an enormous butter-making industry to develop all over the world.

The modern separator is a very efficient machine. Capacities vary from ten gallons per hour to 1500 gallons per hour. A separator, managed efficiently, should extract all but .05% fat from the separated milk.

Cream comes out of the top outlet of the separator and the separated milk from the lower one.

The lower capacity separators are useful for cream production on the farm, and can be a sound investment. All sizes of separators can be driven by electricity. If this is not available, hand turning is easy with the small machines. A highly geared machine such as a separator lasts longer if power is applied evenly. Even application of power is more positive when electricity is used.

Separators are manufactured by dairy engineering firms, and all details for their erection and maintenance are supplied by the makers of the machine. It is very important that the separator should be on a firm level base. This fundamental point is sometimes overlooked, especially when small separators are fixed to the tables. Constant oiling is very important, and the oil used should be special 'separator oil'.

The separator must be correctly assembled before use. Maximum speed must be attained before the milk is allowed to enter the machine. After use, all parts of the machine that come into contact with the milk must be dismantled and washed in warm water, and finally sterilised with boiling water or steam. When not in use, the separator parts must be kept covered in order to avoid contamination. The mechanical separator will last for many years if carefully handled. It is advisable to purchase a separator of slightly larger capacity than needed. Price variations are proportionately small, and time is saved when operating the machine. For example, if 10 gallons of milk are available for cream production, a separator with a capacity of 20 gallons an hour will reduce the operation to half an hour. This point is especially significant when the machine is turned by hand.

The condition of the milk used for separating

The best temperature for separating is 98°-110°F. At this temperature range the fat in the milk is soft and will flow out as cream. The outlet for the cream is small, so cold hard fat may clog up this outlet, and consequently prevent efficient separation. Milk can be separated as soon as it leaves the cow, before the animal heat has been lost. If the temperature of the milk drops, as may occur in colder seasons of the year, the milk must be warmed before entering the separator. Milk which is acid and slightly curdled cannot be separated successfully. The curdled milk clogs up the cream and separated milk outlets. Sour milk is better left until a solid curd is formed and then made into acid-curd cheese. Colostrum, produced for the first 48 hours after the calf is born, does not separate easily. It is advisable to avoid using this product for cheese, butter, or cream until five days after calving.

There are many advantages in separating milk. The economic one is that the maximum amount of fat is extracted from the milk. Separated milk, if left standing for 12 hours or longer, should have no trace of cream on the surface. The presence of a thin layer of cream on separated milk shows faulty working of the machine. The solids of separated milk are valuable food for stock. This food value may be disputed, because the fat content is less than in hand-skimmed milk. This is true, but cheaper vegetable fats can be added to balance it. Separated milk has the same household uses as skimmed milk. Some invalids and infants have difficulty in assimilating milk fat; in such cases separated milk is a valuable source of protein food.

The cream is in a fresh condition for cooling and immediate sale. Cream of varying fat contents can be obtained. There is a special device known as the cream screw fixed on the cream outlet of the separator, which controls the consistency of the cream.

Clotted and scalded cream can be produced from separated cream. A small proportion of separated milk can be poured into the pan in which the cream is to be scalded. The separated cream can be carefully poured back on to the top of this milk. There are practical advantages in this method apart from the saving of time— the chief one being that a larger quantity of cream can be scalded on the milk. Scalded and clotted cream so produced can be of good quality and compare favourably with that produced from gravity methods of cream raising. The fat, left in the skimmed milk after the clotted cream layer has been removed, can be recovered by separation.

Method of separating

1. Assemble machine.
2. Attain maximum speed before the milk enters the machine.
3. Adjust temperature of milk to 98°-110°F.
4. Pour a little warm water through the machine before the milk enters it. This warms up the metal to the temperature of the milk.
5. Maintain full speed throughout the process.
6. Remove source of power immediately all the milk has been separated.
7. Rinse the machine with separated milk or warm water while still revolving. This facilitates later cleaning.
8. Allow the separator to run down completely before dismantling.

9. Dismantle all parts and wash in warm water. Sterilise and store in a clean atmosphere until re-assembled for use.

Cream* can be marketed as heat treated or untreated. Clotted cream should contain not less than 55% milk fat; double cream not less than 48% milk fat and single cream not less than 18% milk fat. Cartons containing the cream must bear the description appropriate, e.g. Clotted Cream, Pasteurised, U.H.T. or untreated. Sterilised and tinned cream cannot easily be made under farmhouse conditions. Their processes of manufacture are complicated and involve large-sized apparatus and scientific control of all operations.

Whipped cream

The fluffy condition of this cream is produced by whisking the cream in a basin. Air is incorporated and the fat globules partially clump. A stable product results as the protein and fat holds the air in the whipped cream. Over-whipped cream will form butter, as the clumping of fat globules will proceed too far. Cream for whipping should be thick in consistency, with a fat content of not less than 35%. The temperature of the cream must be low, 45°-55°F.

Conditions under which cream will not whip

Too high temperature of the cream
Cream too thin
Excessively thick cream, 70-80% fat
Homogenised cream

*See British Cream Regulations 1970, Statutory Instruments No 752.

The process of homogenisation is used commercially for the purpose of giving a thicker consistency to thin cream. The cream so treated is forced under pressure through a machine called an homogeniser. The pressure varies and as much as 2000 lbs. per square inch may be used. This results in the constituents of milk being disintegrated and dispersed. The fat will not subsequently reclump to form either whipped cream or butter. Homogenisation is used for sterilised milk sold in sealed bottles. Milk used in large restaurants is frequently homogenised. No cream line forms on milk so treated. The fat globules are so disintegrated that they no longer respond to the force of gravity, but are evenly dispersed throughout the bulk of the liquid.

Cream 'cheese'

This is produced from thick cream, drained, salted and packaged. It is a cream product and not a true 'cheese'. It contains a high fat portion, varying from 40-70%.

Double and single cream cheese

Cream containing 50-60% fat is used for double cream cheese. It must be cooled after separating to 50°F. and salt added in the proportion of 3 oz. salt : 1 gallon cream. The cream used may be sweet or acid. Cream may be left to sour naturally, or inoculated with starter.

Twelve hours after production the cream should be poured into a thick linen cloth. One cloth 30-36 inches square will hold one gallon of cream. The four corners of the cloth should be pulled up together, and by means of a string, with a slip knot, the cloth forms a bag for the cream. This can be suspended over a basin to allow the surplus liquid to drain from it. The drainage can be hastened by opening the bag of cream and scraping the cream from the outside of the cloth, to allow further liquid to escape. A table knife can be used for scraping. This should be done at intervals of 4-5 hours. Low temperatures of 45°-55°F.(not below 40°F.) are necessary in order to harden the fats. These temperatures are difficult to achieve during the summer months. The coolest place should be chosen for drainage, with draughts of cold air. Old literature describes methods of suspending cream cheese down a well, or burying it in the ground, in order to obtain low temperatures for hardening the fats.

Refrigerator conditions during drainage are not desirable. The fat hardens excessively and the water and protein do not drain out of the curd. The result is that when returned to ordinary temperature, milky deposits seep from the cream cheeses. They can be safely stored in a refrigerator *after* drainage has been completed.

Single cream cheese is produced from a thinner cream and rennet is added. It is recommended when there is no means of cooling the fat, this varying between 20-40%. The higher protein content of the thinner cream makes rennet coagulation possible. Rennet should be added in the proportion of ½ dm rennet : 1 gallon cream. The temperature of the cream should be 75°-80°F. A semi-solid coagulum will be produced in 2-3 hours. This should be ladled into a linen cloth and hung up for drainage, at a temperature of 60°F. for the first 24 hours. This temperature is necessary to allow contraction of the curd by rennet action, which effects drainage of moisture. After 24 hours a large proportion of moisture will have drained from the renneted cream. It should be scraped down as for the double cream cheese, and subsequently kept at as low a temperature as possible, 40°-50°F., in order to harden the fats.

Double and single cream cheeses are ready for consumption when sufficiently drained to give them a solid consistency. Under normal conditions they are ready after 48 hours of drainage. There is no standard method of packing this cheese: waxed boxes, cartons and foil cups can be used. The old-fashioned method of packing was to wrap it in butter muslin. The muslin wrapping is not as hygienic as modern containers, as moulds grow easily on a damp muslin surface. Cream cheese is sold in rectangular and round shapes, weighing two, four and eight ounces. For home consumption a round metal lid from a cocoa or similar tin can be used to shape the cream cheese. This must be lined with greaseproof paper or muslin, otherwise the cheese will stick to the metal.

Double cream cheese will yield 30-36 four ounce cheeses to one gallon of cream. Single cream cheese will yield 20-25 four ounce cheeses to one gallon of cream.

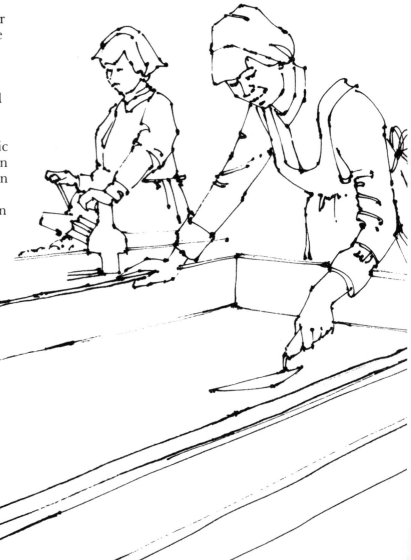

6 BUTTER

Butter-making at home or on the farm must be considered in relation to the economic conditions of milk production. It can be a profitable method of handling surplus milk.

It is important that the available water supply is pure. In the process of butter manufacture water comes into direct contact with the butter. Contaminated water can be a source of danger. Mains water supplies are safe to use, also water from a very deep well. The latter has the advantage of maintaining low temperature at all seasons of the year.

The basic principles of butter production are similar both for farmhouse and creamery manufacture. The composition of butter is:

Water	12-16%
Fat	80-85%
Protein	0.2-0.5%
Salt	1-2%

Butter is usually produced from cream, by the subjection of cream to some form of concussion, or friction. This causes the fat globules to clump together and finally break away from the milk serum. The fat separates out from it in the form of butter granules.

Cream is used for butter making because the butter grains form more easily owing to the concentration of fat, and less space and energy are required for the process. 2½ gallons of milk, containing 3.5% fat will produce one quart of cream, and this cream will yield one pound of butter or nearly 500g.

The churning of whole milk was practised on many farms as late as the nineteenth century. It was customary to collect the milk for several days, in the large butter churn, until the milk soured and became thick or 'loppered'. It was then churned at intervals. The·motive power for the large churn was supplied by a horse, donkey, or a dog on a treadmill. The bulk handled was inevitably cumbersome. The churning of whole milk produced an excellent buttermilk, as it contained all the milk constituents, other than the fat, and was very nutritious. The buttermilk was sold locally, and was very popular.

Butter can be made from cream that has been produced by any of the methods previously described. Its economic aspect is the same as for cream production, cows giving milk containing a high fat percentage being the most profitable.

The quality of the butter is dependent on the treatment that the cream receives between its production and its manufacture into butter. Good quality butter can be made from sweet cream, clotted and scalded cream, or from soured cream.

The sweet cream yields a mild creamy flavoured butter. The clotted and scalded cream butter acquires the characteristic flavour of the heated creams. The soured or ripened cream produces butter with a fuller flavour. Sour or ripened cream, when ready for making

into butter, should have a clean acid taste and smell, with no trace of rancidity or other off flavours. Farmhouse butter-making was traditionally part of the work of the farmer's wife, and was fitted in with farm and household duties. Very small quantities of cream may be produced and churned daily. In this instance the cream is always sweet, and may be raw, or one of the heated creams.

Where larger quantities of cream are retained for butter-making it is advisable to collect the cream, and churn it twice weekly. Under normal conditions of milk and cream production, cream is collected for three or four days, and stored in sound, well-sterilised containers. It should be kept at a temperature of 50°-60°F. and be stirred at intervals. A clean acid flavour is likely to develop in this cream. All the cream for one batch of butter should be mixed together at least twelve hours before it is churned. This ensures an even flavour and temperature throughout the bulk of the cream.

Good butter cannot be made from off-flavoured cream. The chief causes of undesirable flavours in cream collected for butter-making are:

1. Taints in the milk and cream derived from the food fed to the cow, or from strong flavoured plants eaten in the pastures.

2. Flavours absorbed by storing the cream near strong-smelling substances, such as onions.

3. Off-flavours, frequently combined with rancidity, produced by micro-organisms which may gain access to the milk and cream at any point during milk production or subsequent cream handling. In the case of cows with inflammatory conditions of the udder the

micro-organisms may be present before the milk is drawn from the udder. These undesirable flavours produced by micro-organisms increase in intensity with the storage of milk and cream, and their eradication is difficult.

The first investigations for the source of any trouble should be in the dairy. Extra attention should be given to the routine of milk production, especially to the cleanliness of all utensils coming into contact with the milk. Cloths and brushes should be boiled for ten minutes, or soaked in hypochlorite. The utensils used for cream and butter-making must be thoroughly cleaned, and sterilised with boiling water. They should not be wiped with a cloth. The wooden utensils are difficult to clean. If they retain any undesirable smell they should be scrubbed with detergent, or some well-known scourer, followed by rinsing with hot water, and finally boiling water. At all times especial care should be taken in the washing and sterilising of wooden utensils, in order to keep them free from grease or any discolouration. Wood is excellent for temperature control in butter-making, but is quickly contaminated. Woods for butter-making utensils are well seasoned oak, beech and holly wood. The wood must be free from smell. New wooden utensils must be scalded several times before use, or the flavour of the new wood may affect the cream and butter.

Undesirable flavours and taints may persist in the cream after every precaution has been taken. In this case it is advisable to send to a Dairy and Food Technology Department for the culture of lactic micro-organisms known as starter. This product is a culture of micro-organisms grown in sterile milk which will develop in cream and produce a good flavour. Bottles of starter contain about 6-10 oz. of the culture. The contents of the bottle should be stirred into the first quantity of cream to be collected for butter-making, at a minimum temperature of 56°F. As further quantities of cream are produced, each lot should be added and stirred into the cream containing the starter. It is probable that the lactic micro-organisms contained in the starter will overcome those that caused the undesirable flavour.

The addition of starter to raw cream does not always overcome the trouble. In this case the cream must be heated immediately after it is produced to 160°F., then cooled to 60°F., and starter added immediately to the cooled cream. Each subsequent quantity of cream, as soon as produced, must be heated to 160°F. and cooled to 60° before adding to the cream which contains the starter. This procedure is likely to overcome the trouble, as the heating kills those organisms responsible for the undesirable flavour.

A small proportion of the cream, correctly ripened with the starter, can be used to inoculate the next batch of cream to be collected for churning. Approximately half a pint of soured cream is added to ten pints of cream collected for churning, the amount varying with the atmospheric temperature.

It is essential to note the smell and taste of cream to be used for butter-making. A new supply of starter should be bought if any undesirable smell or taint develops. Organisms producing a clean acid souring of cream develop slowly at temperatures below 55°F. When acid cream is preferred for butter-making it must be kept at a temperature of 55°-60°F. If unripened cream is required for butter-making, the cream should be kept as cold as possible. Refrigerators can be used but the temperature must not be below 36°-40°F. The control of temperature is an important factor in all methods of butter-making, and it is advisable to have a thermometer for assessing temperatures.

Using small quantities of cream for butter-making (1-2 pints)

The apparatus required for small quantities of cream is available in most households.

Method Adjust the temperature to 50°-55°F. (The cream should be of such consistency that it will pour.) Pour the cream into a large basin and stir vigorously. A geared egg-whisk is a good implement for this purpose, but a table fork can be used.

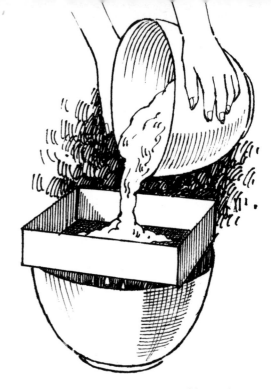

The butter grains and buttermilk can be separated by pouring through a hair sieve.

The cream in the basin must be stirred or whisked vigorously until the butter grains begin to appear.

Cease stirring when grains of butter are formed; this takes approximately 10-15 minutes. Place a piece of muslin or a hair-sieve over a second basin and pour the butter and buttermilk into it, thus separating the butter from the buttermilk. The grains of butter held in the sieve or cloth can then by rinsed free from buttermilk by holding under a tap of running cold water, until milkiness disappears. Water at a temperature of 48°-50°F. keeps the butter fat firm and easy to handle. After washing, press the butter granules together by means of a rolling pin and board. Roll five or six times. Before using, scald wooden implements with boiling water, and cool with cold water, to prevent the butter sticking to the dry wood.

Sprinkle salt on to the butter while rolling it. The proportion of salt varies with taste –¼ oz salt : 1 pound butter gives a slightly salted product.

Alternative apparatus for home butter production

(*a*) Small glass churns.
(*b*) Screw top fruit bottling jars.

The small glass churns are turned with a handle, or have small beaters rotating inside the churn. Half to one pound of butter can be made in them.

The cream in fruit bottling jars can be agitated by shaking. The glass churns and jars should never be filled more than one third of their capacity as if too full, concussion and friction is checked and butter production retarded. As in the basin and whisk method, the temperature and consistency of the cream should be controlled. The butter should be handled in the granular state to remove the buttermilk, and then pressed to remove moisture and to mix in the salt.

Butter made by any of these simple methods has a very limited keeping quality, and should be consumed within one or two days of production.

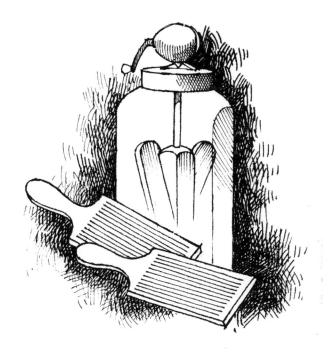

By turning the handle on the glass butter churn the small paddles or beaters agitate the cream until butter grains form. The grooved wooden implements are Scotch hands, for working the butter.

Making larger quantities of butter—4 lb. or more

Special apparatus is needed when handling one gallon or more of cream for butter-making. This consists of:

(*a*) A butter churn. This is traditionally made of wood. There are various types on the market. One of the easiest to manipulate is the end-over-end barrel type, with a clip-on lid. The cream is formed into butter in the churn.

(b) Small utensils such as Scotch hands (these are made of grooved wood and are used for handling the butter—originally called scotched hands). Butter scoops, a sieve, squeegee and butter muslin.

Method All dry wooden utensils must be prepared for use by scalding with boiling water and immediately cooling with cold water. They must be kept wet until used. This treatment of the wood prevents the cream and butter from sticking to it.

The churn should be rinsed out with water at a temperature between 50°-60°F. This is the temperature range used for hand churning, the lower temperatures in the hot weather and the higher temperatures in cold weather. Average churning temperatures are 52°-54°F.

The cream for butter-making should not be too thick (30% fat). It should flow easily off a Scotch hand. The consistency can be adjusted by the addition of cold water. The temperatures of the cream should be the same as that of the churn—between 50°-60°F. If the cream is the correct consistency and temperature, and the churn not more than one third full, the churning time should not exceed 10-15 minutes. The revolving of the churn should be done evenly. A small valve is fixed to the churns, which should be pressed down at intervals during the churning of the cream. The purpose of this ventilator is to maintain even pressure inside the churn. The pressure increases because natural gases are liberated from the cream as it forms into butter, and if not released by the ventilator the increased pressure may cause the plug of the churn to be forced out, causing a wastage of cream.

The indicator glass will show when the cream thickens, and the churn feels heavier to handle. At this stage it is turned more slowly. Finally small butter granules will appear on the glass. The butter must be kept in granules and this can be controlled by adding water, if possible 4-6° lower than churning temperature, to the buttermilk in the churn, until butter grains about the size of grains of wheat are produced. If granules are allowed to form into lumps, elimination of buttermilk is difficult, and the keeping quality of butter is reduced. The buttermilk is removed through the plug hole of the churn and should be replaced by an equal amount of water at a temperature of 50°F. The butter is churned several times in this washing water. The first washing water is removed and the process repeated with fresh cold water and the butter churned for a short time. The second washing water should come out of the churn quite clear, denoting that the butter grains have been washed free of buttermilk, and will consequently keep longer than unwashed or overchurned butter. It is possible to add the second washing water in the form of brine. Butter salted by this method can only be slightly salted. Brining butter has two main advantages:

1. No streakiness occurs in the butter from uneven salting.

2. Salt dissolved in water reduces the temperature of the water three or four degrees, an asset in hot weather.

The brine should be of 10% strength—that is approximately 1 lb. salt : 1 gallon water, and made in sufficient quantity to float the butter grains. They should be left in the brine 10-15 minutes.

84

The temperature of the final washing water, or brine, should be regulated to approximately 50°F. At this temperature the butter is of sufficiently firm consistency to handle when placed on the draining table by means of a wooden scoop.

The butter table should be rinsed down with water or brine at the same temperature as that of the churn. Any marked difference in temperature between the butter and the wood will cause the butter to 'stick' during the working process.

The butter is handled during working by means of the Scotch hands. The butter is worked in order to expel moisture and to distribute the water droplets evenly in the butter fat, and to

Working the butter between the Scotch hands expels water. Scotch hands are also the tools for making large or small butter rolls.

consolidate the butter. Butter for sale must not legally contain more than 16% moisture. Farmhouse butter on an average contains 13-14% moisture, if rolled five or six times on the butter table. The moisture should be mopped up with a clean muslin during the process.

Well worked butter should have a close texture, and be firm to handle. When pressed between Scotch hands clear droplets of water should be evenly distributed throughout the bulk. Heavily salted butter can be produced by adding salt, through a sifter, to the butter during the working process. The proportion varies, ¼-½ oz. salt : 1 pound butter. The salt used must be of good quality and free from lumps. Uneven salting is a common cause of streakiness in farmhouse butter.

Butter prints and packaging

Butter made for sale in pound or metric quantities should be attractively shaped. This is frequently done by making the butter into bricks with the Scotch hands, and covering the upper surface with a printed design. Some makers prefer to market their butter in rolls—this can be done by flattening the weighed portion of butter and rolling it on to itself. Wooden prints can be bought for patterning the butter. Motifs such as swans, ears of wheat, and flowers, are traditional in butter print designs. The printing and shaping of butter was the pride of the good butter-maker who established a particular design on the butter—an early form of trade mark.

Many market towns have a Butter Market. This is a relic of the days when farmers' wives brought their butter into the market each week. The butter was sold on cabbage and rhubarb leaves. At Bramhill in Wiltshire there is a statue to Maud Heath. She holds a butter basket and looks over the vale to Chippenham, four miles away. Maud Heath walked into Chippenham

weekly with her butter, over a waterlogged track. When she died she left all her savings with instructions that a causeway should be built in order that women trudging to market should in future have a good pathway. Some years after her death that causeway was built, and there are more than sixty supporting brick archways which raise the path above the marsh.

Butter can be shaped into any form for table decoration, but can only be handled for decorative work if it is firm in texture, at temperatures of 45°-50°F.

Butter should be wrapped in good quality vegetable parchment or waxed paper and stood in a refrigerator or cold larder until used.

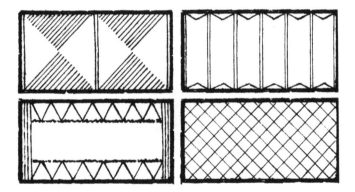

A selection of patterns on bricks of butter, made with Scotch hands or with wooden butter prints.

Washing up and maintenance of utensils

The washing of wooden utensils is important. Hot water must be used to remove all fat from the wood, and vigorous scrubbing is essential.

After the first washing, boiling water should be poured over all wooden apparatus, and this should result in quick drying of the hot wood. If cloths or muslins are used for drying off the moisture they must be clean and must be boiled after each using. Wooden butter churns and workers not in use will become too dry and therefore crack unless swelled with warm water at intervals. Water should not, however, be kept permanently on the churns and workers, or mould contaminants will grow on the wood; alternate soaking and drying is the only way of keeping these utensils in good conditions when not in constant use.

Judging farmhouse butter

The product is usually exhibited in pound, half pound, or metric blocks. The judge should examine these staged bricks, rolls or whatever type of representation is stated by the show schedule, and mark in the first place for general appearance, effect of packaging etc. The colour of the butter should also be assessed. The judge should then take one brick and cut it half way down with a knife, breaking the second half; in this way the texture and 'grain' can be judged. The texture should be close and waxy; the break rough like cast iron, with no apparent air spaces. After assessing these points, the half of the butter showing the texture should be pressed between two Scotch hands, and the visible moisture noted; this should be evenly distributed and quite clear (the less visible moisture present the better). Finally the butter should be tasted. A very small portion should be taken, and preferably not swallowed, as a strong taste on the tasting cells at the back of the tongue may interfere with the taste of subsequent samples. Eating a small portion of plain biscuit, or a piece of apple, between each sampling prevents any confusion of butter flavours. The following are two possible scales of points:

Flavour	50
Texture	20
Colour	10
Apparent moisture	10
Appearance	10
	100

Flavour	50
Moisture and texture	40
Colour and appearance	10
	100

Summary
Successful farmhouse butter manufacture depends on:

1. Clean milk supply—colostrum should never be used for butter-making.
2. Care in handling the cream; whether skimmed or separated, the bulk must be stirred at intervals before churning. Flavour at churning should be good. Churning should be done twice weekly.
3. Clean, well-prepared utensils.
4. Correct consistency and temperature of cream when churned.
5. Churning the butter to a granular state.
6. Washing the butter free from buttermilk.
7. Brining or dry salting butter—with adequate working to expel moisture and consolidate texture.
8. Good packaging in odourless paper and boxes.
9. Adequate sterilisation of all utensils after use.

Common faults of farmhouse butter

Flavour Off-flavour frequently apparent in the cream and due to absorbed taints or the presence of undesirable micro-organisms.

Colour Intensity of colour due to breed of cow, season of the year. Pale butter can be coloured by the vegetable butter colour called annatto, added to the cream immediately before churning. Streakiness denotes careless manipulation of the butter on the worker, or the uneven distribution of dry salt.

Texture Open texture and very uneven distribution of moisture shows inadequate working of the butter, possibly due to too high or too low a temperature of the butter when handled.

Keeping quality Farmhouse butter should keep at a cool room temperature (55°-60°F.) for three weeks, and for longer than this if held at a lower temperature. Keeping quality is lessened by contaminated cream, very over-acid cream, and buttermilk in the butter.

Potted butter

Butter for preservation without deep refrigeration must be made from good flavoured cream produced under the most hygienic conditions. The cream should only be ripened to an acidity of 0.25 to 0.3% and should have a clean, slightly acid taste and smell.

Method Butter for preservation should be churned to rather small grain, washed at least twice, and then brined for 20 minutes. The butter should then be removed from the brine, placed on the butter-worker, and rolled five or six times in order to remove all superfluous moisture. The butter should be left on the worker if possible for 3 or 4 hours and then again rolled five or six times. During this second rolling dry salt should be added in the proportion of about ¾ oz. salt : 1 lb. butter and worked well into the butter, expelling as much moisture as possible. The texture of the butter is much less important than its required low moisture content.

After the second working the butter was traditionally packed into a dry, glazed earthenware crock. The crock must be free from cracks and be well washed and scalded before use. The butter should be filled into the crock very firmly, and there should be no air spaces whatsoever—this can be achieved by working the butter in the crock if large enough from the centre outwards with a piece of clean, damp muslin over the closed fist. Finally the butter should be levelled and covered with a layer of salt two inches thick. The crock should be covered with parchment or greaseproof paper, tied down, and stored in a cool place until the butter is required for use. Butter thus potted should keep for 4-6 months.

If the butter tastes excessively salty when required for use, it should be removed from the crock in pieces about the size of a walnut, allowed to stand in clean water for 30 to 40 minutes, and then re-worked.

Buttermilk

Buttermilk can be fed to stock and used for cooking purposes. Its composition is approximately:

Water	91%
Fat	0.3%
Protein	3.5%
Lactose	4.5%
Ash	0.7%

Buttermilk may contain excessive water, as it is customary to add water to the buttermilk when forming the butter grain. Diluted buttermilk should be left undisturbed for 24 hours, which allows the curdy portion to settle to the bottom of the container. The excess water on the surface can then be poured away and the buttermilk used for household purposes, or cheese-making.

Buttermilk cheese, called Bon Don in some districts, is not economic unless two or more gallons of buttermilk are available.
There are two simple methods of making cheese from buttermilk:

1. *Buttermilk only* The buttermilk must be acid, and if produced from acid cream no further souring is necessary. Buttermilk from sweet cream butter should be left 12 to 36 hours to sour. Starter can be added to it. The soured buttermilk should be heated to a temperature of 160°F. The heating causes the curd to separate from the liquid. The curd settles on the bottom of the container in a soft flocculent mass, which should be left for cooling for two or three hours. This curd can be poured on to a cloth of close texture such as a clean linen tea towel. The water drains through the cloth. The process can be shortened if the cloth is hung up by the four corners to make a hanging bag, and the curd scraped down at intervals as in the case of lactic and cream cheese.

This cheese should drain in 48 hours, resulting in a smooth, soft-textured product. It should be eaten with flavourings such as Marmite, and is good for sandwiches.

2. *Buttermilk and milk* Buttermilk cheese made from half buttermilk and half new milk, or from two-thirds buttermilk and one third new milk.

The temperature of this mixture should be raised to 80-82°F. Rennet should be added in the proportion of 1 dm standard rennet : 3 gallons of the mixture, and well stirred into it. A good coagulum will form in 1-1½ hours. This should be ladled into a linen cloth and treated as in (1). Buttermilk cheese made with new milk added to the buttermilk produces a firm cheese, with a slightly granular texture. The addition of salt to buttermilk cheese is optional.

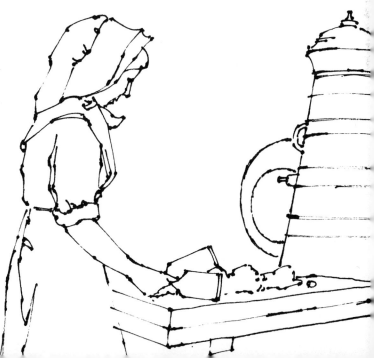

7 OTHER RECIPES

Yorkshire Curd

Sour milk can be used for Yorkshire Curd.

Method 1 The sour milk should be heated to 160°F. The whey separates out and should be strained off. The tough curd is hung up in a muslin bag for two hours until drained.

Method 2 Full cream milk, or separated milk, should be heated to 180°-190°F. At this temperature vinegar*, or sour milk, can be added in the proportion of 1 tablespoonful : 1½ pints of the hot milk. The addition of the acid causes immediate curdling of the protein. The whey separates, and should be strained off, and the curd hung up in a muslin bag for two hours until firm.

Yorkshire Curd is used for making curd cheesecakes. It is a tough curd, and lacks flavour unless mixed with other ingredients. Sugar, butter, eggs, currants, peel, and nutmeg are mixed with the curd, which is then baked brown inside a pastry crust.

* Epsom Salts can be used.

90

Yoghurt

This is a sour milk preparation obtainable from many dairies, and which has gained great popularity in recent years. The cultures of micro-organisms producing the fermentation differ from those used in starter for butter and cheese-making.

The most important of the micro-organisms concerned is the famous *Lactobacillus Bulgaricus,*† so named because of its presence in the original Bulgarian, and other South European and Asiatic soured milks. The therapeutic value to those populations where it formed a staple article of diet led the microbiologist Metchkinoff (1845-1916) to attribute longevity to the influence of the 'Bacillus of Long Life'. The claim is not a true one, but it is proved that yoghurt and allied fermented milks have a

† Yoghurt cultures usually also contain *Strep. thermopholus* and *L. acidophilus*

useful affect in counteracting the toxic effects induced by intestinal disturbances. The presence of large numbers of putrefactive organisms in the intestinal tract may cause the production of poisonous substances which are absorbed by the system. The action of the micro-organisms causing this 'auto-intoxic-ation' is reduced, or prevented, by the large numbers of inoculated lactobacilli, which produce a highly acid condition.

The native and commercial yoghurts have a characteristic dense curd, which can be broken down to a smooth, creamy consistency. The original curds were made from milk partially evaporated in the sun, and the commercial

preparations rely on processes of heat treatment and homogenisation. These methods are not possible in the British home, but the curdled flavour and concentrated consistency of the curd can be obtained by quite simple methods. It must be remembered that yoghurt cultures are not so easy to maintain in a pure state as the ordinary lactic starter, as they are easily contaminated. Supplies should be constantly renewed.

Method 1 Obtain a yoghurt culture. Boil two pints of milk in a double saucepan, simmering it at boiling point for thirty minutes. If using a pressure cooker, time is shorter. Cool the milk, in the pan, by circulation of cold water, to an exact temperature of 113°F. Previously prepare a clean wide-necked vaccuum flask, and pour into it the culture, or the bottle of yoghurt. Cork the flask, and during all operations, avoid entrance of airborne contaminants as far as possible. When the milk is at 113°F. pour it quickly on to the yoghurt in the flask, and re-cork.

The flask maintains the temperature by vacuum insulation (which is very important, as 113°F. is the critical temperature for the growth of yoghurt culture). Leave flask for 6-12 hours, according to the degree of acidity preferred in the curd. When the curd is ready, pour it out of flask, but do not wash the curd remnants off the internal surfaces. The remains of the curd will act as the inoculation for the next lot of boiled, cooled, milk poured into it.

Continue the process daily, but renew cultures if curd becomes gassy, wheyed off, or loses its acidity. Be sure to boil the cork of the thermos before replacing, to avoid contamination by moulds.

Modern yoghurt makers work on the same principles as the Thermos. A small amount of 'plain' yoghurt is placed in the container (the insulated box or the small glass jars) and milk at the critical temperature is added. The container is then closed and the milk hindered from cooling too rapidly (thus preventing curd development) by the insulation of the double walls or by gently regulated heat from an electric element beneath the glass jars.

Method 2. Open a can of evaporated (unsweetened condensed) milk. Dilute with an equal quantity of water. Heat it to 113°F. and pour direct into the flask containing the yoghurt inoculation.

The use of canned evaporated milk is very satisfactory, and not costly. The danger of contamination is reduced. Time is saved. The flavour and texture of the yoghurt curd formed from it is truer to type, having a delicious caramelled flavour, and creamy texture and colour.

Junket

The aim when making junket is to obtain a soft curd, which will not quickly contract and separate into curds and whey. Junket curd should be close in texture, but not tough or 'stringy'. It is best to use junket rennet sold for the purpose, but if cheese rennet is substituted, it must be diluted six times with cold water before measuring out the amount to use.

Causes of contractile curd

Milk at too high a temperature when adding rennet.

Milk too old, or slightly acid.

Too much rennet used.

Causes of a weak sloppy curd

Too low a temperature when adding rennet.

Milk excessively heat-treated.

Insufficient, or old and inactive, rennet.

Junket cannot be made from milk which has previously been boiled, as the high temperature has changed some of the milk constituents, and rennet will no longer act. It cannot be made from sterilised bottled milk, no from canned evaporated milk, as during their preparation they have been subjected to homogenisation and high temperature treatment, both of which prevent the action of rennet.

Method of making junket Heat one pint fresh full-cream milk in a double saucepan to 100°F. Pour warm milk into container from which it is to be served. Mix in thoroughly 1 teaspoonful rennet (1½ teaspoonsful if milk is pasteurised, or if goat's milk is used).

Add sugar to taste, and any flavourings required. Leave container in a warm place for milk to coagulate. Be sure that it is not moved during the setting period, as disturbance of the curd may cause it to flake.

When curd is firm, sprinkle grated nutmeg on the surface. Alternatively, pile on whipped, or clotted, cream.

GLOSSARY

Acid-curd Curd produced by coagulation of casein by acids (normally lactic acid).

Albumen and Globulin Albuminous proteins, coagulated by heat.

Annatto Orange-red dye used to colour cheese.

Antibiotic Chemical substance, of microbial origin, which inhibits the growth or activity of micro-organisms.

Bacteria Minute living vegetable cells.

Casein Chief protein constituent of milk. Coagulated by action of rennet or by acids.

Clean Absence of any taint or 'off-flavour'.

Colostrum The first milk secreted after giving birth.

Contractile curd A firm curd which shrinks and expels the whey.

Creaming Allowing cream to rise by gravity, OR skimming risen cream off surface of milk.

Culture Laboratory-prepared growth of living micro-organisms, e.g.'starter'.

Detergent Chemical substance with dissolving action on milk deposits.

Enzyme Chemical agent, produced by a living cell, minute amounts of which can cause chemical changes in organic matter.

Flocculent curd A soft broken curd with little contractile property.

Fore-milk The milk first drawn from the cow's udder at each milking.

Globulin *see* Albumen

Graded cheese Inspected and stamped in quality grades by authorised grader. Separate schemes in operation for home-produced farmhouse and creamery cheese.

Gravity drainage Natural drainage by force of gravity. No aid by pressure.

Hoop A curd container without a fused base in which curd is drained but not pressed.

Hypochlorite Chemical solution used, after physical cleaning of utensils etc., to destroy micro-organisms.

Inhibitive substances Those which inhibit the growth of micro-organisms.

Lactation Period during which milk is secreted.

Lactic acid fermentation The production of

lactic acid from the lactose (milk sugar) by action of micro-organisms.

Mastitis Inflammatory condition of udder, often due to infection by micro-organisms.

Micro-organisms Minute living vegetable cells, including yeasts, moulds and bacteria.

Mould Living cell, characterised by spore-bearing thread-like growth.

Mould (Cheese) A container with a fused base and fitting followers in which to shape or mould the curd under pressure. Alternative terms: **Chesset, Cheese vat.**

Parturition Birth of an animal.

Pasteurisation Heat-treatment of a substance to a temperature sufficient to destroy micro-organisms, degree of destruction depending on temperature of heating. Named after Pasteur, who originated the control of fermentations by heat action.

Pitched curd Curd settled in the whey.

Raw milk or cream Not subjected to any heat treatment.

Rennet Extract of rennin in brine.

Rennet-curd Curd produced by coagulation of casein by rennin (rennet).

Rennin Enzyme of a digestive juice of mammals, having the specific property of coagulating milk.

Ripening of cheese Period of maturing, during which cheese undergoes chemical changes (chiefly proteolysis) by action of micro-organisms.

Ripening of milk Development of lactic acidity previous to renneting.

Salts of milk (Mineral matter or Ash) Chiefly composed of phosphates, chlorides, and citrates of calcium, sodium, magnesium, and potassium. Also traces of metals.

Spore (Mould) Reproductive bodies or 'seeds'.

Starter Liquid cultures used to ensure the presence of lactic acid-producing organisms.

Sterilisation Treatment by dry or wet heat to high temperature, or by chemicals, to destroy all micro-organisms.

Stringy curd Tough and elastic, generally by action of heat or acidity.

Strippings The milk last drawn from the udder at each milking.

Sweet milk Low content of lactic acid.

Taint or off-flavour Any substances giving a bad flavour to milk and its products.

Wheyed-off Free whey escaping from a curd.

Yeast Living cell (larger than bacterial cell) which ferments sugar.

SUPPLIERS

Much of the equipment needed for cheese, cream, or butter making can be found already in the home, or easily obtained from household or hardware stores.

All cheese and butter making equipment: Self-sufficiency and Smallholding Supplies, The Old Palace, Priory Road, Wells, Somerset.

Starter can be bought from Hansen's Laboratories, Thornbury Trading Estate, Thornbury, Glos, *or* from Unigate Ltd., Trowbridge, Wilts, *or* from county colleges of Agriculture (addresses in telephone directories).

Separators: look under Dairy Engineers in the Classified Directory.

Insulated flask yoghurt makers obtainable from Deva Bridge Ltd., P.O. Box 5, Stowmarket, Suffolk.

Electric type: electrical suppliers.

CONVERSION TABLES

C	F	C	F	C	F	C	F	C	F
1	33.8	21	69.8	41	105.8	61	141.8	81	177.8
2	35.6	22	71.6	42	107.6	62	143.6	82	179.6
3	37.4	23	73.4	43	109.4	63	145.4	83	181.4
4	39.2	24	75.2	44	111.2	64	147.2	84	183.2
5	41.0	25	77.0	45	113.0	65	149.0	85	185.0
6	42.8	26	78.8	46	114.8	66	150.8	86	186.8
7	44.6	27	80.6	47	116.6	67	152.6	87	188.6
8	46.4	28	82.4	48	118.4	68	154.4	88	190.4
9	48.2	29	84.2	49	120.2	69	156.2	89	192.2
10	50.0	30	86.0	50	122.0	70	158.0	90	194.0
11	51.8	31	87.8	51	123.8	71	159.8	91	195.8
12	53.6	32	89.6	52	125.6	72	161.6	92	197.0
13	55.5	33	91.4	53	127.4	73	163.4	93	199.0
14	57.2	34	93.2	54	129.2	74	165.2	94	201.2
15	59.0	35	95.0	55	131.0	75	167.0	95	203.0
16	60.8	36	96.8	56	132.8	76	168.8	96	204.8
17	62.6	37	98.6	57	134.6	77	170.6	97	206.6
18	64.4	38	100.4	58	136.4	78	172.4	98	208.4
19	66.2	39	102.2	59	138.2	79	174.2	99	210.2
20	68.0	40	104.0	60	140.0	80	176.0	100	212.0

(Temperature in degrees F - 32) $\times \frac{5}{9}$ = degrees Celsius.
(Temperature in degrees C $\times \frac{9}{5}$) + 32 = degrees Fahrenheit.

Weight

16 drachms	=	1oz.
16 oz.	=	1lb.
1 oz.	=	28.35 grams
1 lb.	=	453.6 grams
	=	0.4536 kilos
2.2 lb.	=	1 kilo

Liquid measure

60 minims or 'drops'	=	1 fluid drachm
	=	3.5 millilitres
	=	1 teaspoonful
8 fluid drachms	=	1 fluid oz.
	=	2 tablespoonsful
20 fluid oz.	=	1 pint
	=	0.57 litre
1 litre	=	1.76 pints (approx)
1 gallon	=	4.546 litres

Length

1 inch	=	2.54 centimetres
	=	25.4 millimetres
1 foot	=	30.48 centimetres
	=	304.8 millimetres
1 yard	=	0.914 metres